ON THE LEDGE

Alan Bleasdale was born in Liverpool and, apart from three years teaching in the Gilbert and Ellice Islands, has always lived on Merseyside. Since leaving teaching in 1975 he has written two novels, a feature film, numerous short stories, eleven stage plays, six television plays and four television series.

In 1983 the five-part television series *The Boys from the Black Stuff* gained Alan Bleasdale a BAFTA award, the Pye Television Award and the Broadcasting Press Guild Television Award as the Writer of the Year. Other television credits include *The Muscle Market*, *Scully* and *The Monocled Mutineer*. His feature film *No Surrender* won the 1984 Critics' Award at the Toronto Film Festival.

His work for the theatre includes *Fat Harold and the Last 26*, *Down the Dock Road*, *It's a Madhouse*, *No More Sitting on the Old School Bench* and *Are You Lonesome Tonight?* (Evening Standard Best Musical award, 1985). *Having a Ball* broke all box office records at the Liverpool Playhouse in 1990 before transferring to the West End and touring thereafter.

His controversial seven-part Channel Four series *GBH* won the 1991 Broadcasting Press Guild Television Award.

ON THE LEDGE
Alan Bleasdale

faber and faber
LONDON · BOSTON

First published in Great Britain in 1993 by
Faber and Faber Limited
3 Queen Square London WC1N 3AU

Photoset by Parker Typesetting Service, Leicester
Printed in England by Clays Ltd, St Ives plc

A CIP record for this book is available from the British
Library.

ISBN 0-571-17062-5

2 4 6 8 10 9 7 5 3 1

On the Ledge, a joint Nottingham Playhouse and Royal National Theatre production, was first performed at the Nottingham Playhouse on 23 February 1993 and at the Lyttelton Theatre, London, on 27 April 1993. The cast was as follows:

UPRIGHT	Mark McGann
UPSIDE DOWN	Jacob Abraham
MAL	Dearbhla Molloy
MAN ON THE LEDGE	David Ross
FIRST BRUTE	Paul Broughton
SECOND BRUTE	Alan Igbon
SHAUN	Jimmy Mulville
MOEY	Gary Olsen
MARTIN	Christopher Ryan
Director	Robin Lefevre
Designer	William Dudley
Lighting	Nick Chelton

'You've got to have fuck-off money,
which I think is the only thing that matters.'
Alan Whicker

'Fuck off.'
Edwina Currie, to an NHS surgeon

'Read it with the ear.'
Gerard Manley Hopkins

ACT ONE

*The exterior of a block of flats. A flat roof and railings visible. We can
see both the top and the next-to-top floors of the flats.
A ledge runs along each floor. Wide rectangular windows on each
floor. Some may be boarded up. There are a couple of dead Sky dishes
attached to the outer wall.
Two lads in their late teens are on the flat roof. One is being held
upside down over the railings by the ankles by the other lad. The
upside-down lad has a pot of paint in one hand and a paintbrush in the
other. He is completing the legend 'ANACHRY RULES' (sic).*

UPSIDE DOWN: . . . London, hey?

UPRIGHT: (*Sourly*) Yeah, London.

UPSIDE DOWN: I wondered where you'd been.

UPRIGHT: I'm not goin' again. The bastards hate us.

UPSIDE DOWN: But what's it really like down South?

UPRIGHT: I don't know. I wasn't there long enough.

UPSIDE DOWN: Y've been gone a year. At least.

UPRIGHT: But I was only down there six months . . . (*Very
thoughtfully*) . . . before the bastards got me . . . bastard
Cockney police . . . bastard Cockney courtroom . . . bastard
Cockney jury . . . bastard Cockney barristers . . . bastard
Cockney judge –

UPSIDE DOWN: The judge was a Cockney?

UPRIGHT: (*Oblivious*) – Bastard Cockney detention centre –
bastard Cockney police escort up the bastard Cockney M1
. . . bastard nine months in Wakefield gaol . . . no time off
for good behaviour because I wouldn't bastard well behave
. . . bastard Edwina Currie.

UPSIDE DOWN: I know . . . What? Edwina Currie?

UPRIGHT: It's all her fault, her and that bastard Peter Bastard
Sissons and all the other bastards on his bastard *Question
Time* . . . because of them, the bastard I was robbin' turned
his bastard telly off.

UPSIDE DOWN: D'you blame him?

UPRIGHT: Came in the bastard back-kitchen, didn't he, the Cockney bastard, and bastard well caught me . . . bastard black eye . . . bastard broken nose, broken bones, bastard boot in the balls . . . bastard frostbite –

UPSIDE DOWN: Frostbite?

UPRIGHT: I'm comin' to that . . . bastard hospital . . . bastard intensive care.

UPSIDE DOWN: Was he a big bastard?

UPRIGHT: Bastard body builder . . . If I'd been thinking straight, if I'd have been a proper robber, I'd have realized – I'd just robbed his fuckin' Bullworker . . .

UPSIDE DOWN: Typical.

(UPRIGHT *looks down. Contemplates. Grins.*)

UPRIGHT: . . . Still get like, y'know, side effects.

UPSIDE DOWN: Oh yeah? Like what?

UPRIGHT: Oh nothin', just me wrists sometimes give way on me. Without warnin'.

(*He shakes* UPSIDE DOWN *by the ankles, and ruins the 'R' in 'RULES'.*)

UPSIDE DOWN: Y'bastard!

UPRIGHT: I know. Still, it had a sort of happy ending . . . I might have got nine months but that bastard body builder got three and a half years for attempted murder. Serves him fuckin' well right. I'm tellin' y', he was fuckin' deranged; it's no fun bein' locked in a fuckin' big chest freezer, y'know . . . I'll never forget lyin' there on the floor with his foot on me throat while he's emptyin' it out, screamin', 'Die, y' Scouse bastard!', fuckin' frozen sprouts and tubs of ice-cream bouncin' all around me . . . and then fuck off, into his freezer . . . the police had to wait until I was defrosted before they could interview me . . . still be there now if his wife hadn't come home and told him the cost of letting frozen sirloin steak go to waste.

UPSIDE DOWN: (*Cockney*) 'Got anything in the freezer, girl?'

UPRIGHT: (*Cockney*) 'Only that fuckin' thief you caught last year, Eric.'

UPSIDE DOWN: (*Cockney*) 'Put him in the microwave, let's have some Scouse.'

(*They both laugh.* UPSIDE DOWN *is finishing off the 'S' in*
'*RULES*'.)

UPRIGHT: . . . Life's a bastard, all right. That's what life is.

UPSIDE DOWN: It's finished now.

(UPSIDE DOWN *puts the paint brush in the pot.*)

UPRIGHT: Don't depress me, Billy. Not at my age. I'm depressed
enough. Life might be a bastard but don't tell me it's
finished.

UPSIDE DOWN: No –

UPRIGHT: That's why I went down South.

(UPRIGHT *becomes impassioned.* UPSIDE DOWN *gets shaken
about.*)

I wasn't goin' down there to thieve. Was I fuck. I was just
goin' down there to you know like *achieve* – ended up in
Hammersmith. Under the bastard bridge.

UPSIDE DOWN: Listen –

UPRIGHT: Open y'mouth down there – y'fuckin' accent stands up
in court an' pleads guilty on y'behalf. No wonder the bastard
Cockneys call it y'North an' South. Pretended to be from
Scotland.

UPSIDE DOWN: *Jimmy, f'fuck's sake, will y'listen to me!*

(UPRIGHT *lets go of* UPSIDE DOWN *with one hand and points
an admonishing finger at him.*)

UPRIGHT: Don't interrupt. It's bad manners to interrupt.

(UPSIDE DOWN *dangles one leg free until* UPRIGHT, *his dignity
and position firmly established, takes hold of both ankles again.*)

Anyway, I pretended I was from Glasgow once, 'cos it was
the only other accent I could do – 'Och aye, the fuckin' noo,
Jimmy.'

UPSIDE DOWN: *Jimmy!*

UPRIGHT: I should have known – the bastards don't like the
Jocks neither.

UPSIDE DOWN: No no, listen to me, it's me paintin', that's what's
finished. An' I'm goin' all dizzy! Get me up will y'!

UPRIGHT: I went after a flat in Croydon one day. And . . . and . . .
and . . . I didn't get it.

(UPRIGHT *slumps forward over the railing.* UPSIDE DOWN
lurches further down.)

3

UPSIDE DOWN: Jimmy, I don't wanna go down. I wanna go up.

UPRIGHT: In the world. I know. So do I. Up, up and away.

UPSIDE DOWN: D'you think you could start with me first?

UPRIGHT: What? . . . Oh aye yeah. I almost forgot you were there.

UPSIDE DOWN: . . . Fuckin' hell . . . What shall I do with the paint and that?

UPRIGHT: Who cares.

 (UPSIDE DOWN *drops the paint pot and the brush.*)

 . . . Well, someone's just got a two-tone Ford Cortina.

 (UPSIDE DOWN *climbs back to safety.*)

 What's that y've put?

UPSIDE DOWN: (*With pride*) Lean over, have a look for yourself.

UPRIGHT: Er no, y'all right, just tell us what y've put.

UPSIDE DOWN: 'Anarchy Rules.' Neat, hey?

UPRIGHT: Oh yeah, deffo beats 'Macker is a Wanker' . . . But what is it, this anarchy lark?

UPSIDE DOWN: It's er y'know, when there's sort of no rules or nothin', well, there are rules like, but everyone ignores them, an' everythin's kind of all fucked up.

UPRIGHT: (*Seriously*) . . . So it's sort of like everyday life?

UPSIDE DOWN: No. I don't think so, anyway. No it's not. It's like this bloke was explainin' to me in the library –

UPRIGHT: *The library? You?*

UPSIDE DOWN: Yeah, it was pissin' down outside. But he was sayin' – until we got told to shut up – but he said he wouldn't shut up 'cos he was an anarchist – and then we got thrown out of the library, and in the chippy he said it was doin' things on purpose, this anarchy, you know, refusin' to obey. Deliberate. By the people. With no hope. An' if you did that, it was your only hope. Like.

UPRIGHT: Huh, who cares?

UPSIDE DOWN: I think it might be that as well. Not carin' any more, you know, fuck it. Like . . . He bought me me chips.

UPRIGHT: He must have been after y'arse.

UPSIDE DOWN: No, he wasn't. He was an anarchist, not an arsonist.

 (*They both fall about laughing.*)

4

UPRIGHT: You're the same age as me, aren't y'?

UPSIDE DOWN: Yeah.

UPRIGHT: It's terrible, isn't it?

UPSIDE DOWN: (*Uneasily*) Well . . . it's a bit old like, isn't it? Or it was when I was . . . younger. It seemed old I suppose when I was five, but I didn't really like . . . worry about it . . . when I was five.

UPRIGHT: But it is terrible, isn't it? Isn't it . . .? *Isn't it?*

UPSIDE DOWN: Er, yeah. Oh aye, yeah. Terrible. Fuckin' dreadful. I don't know how I cope most days.

UPRIGHT: I thought as much. I knew I wasn't alone.

UPSIDE DOWN: Er, tell y'what – it's Bommie Night, let's go down to one of the bonfires, hey?

UPRIGHT: Y'can't. Y'at that age now. Y'd get laughed at. That's what I mean about it bein' –

BOTH: Terrible.

UPSIDE DOWN: I know, but I wasn't exactly plannin' on bringin' me sparklers with me, chantin' 'Build a bonfire –

BOTH: Build a Bonfire,
    Put the teachers at the top,
    Put the Headmaster in the middle,
    And burn the bloomin' lot!'

(UPSIDE DOWN *laughs.* UPRIGHT *smacks the railing with his hand*.)

UPRIGHT: (*Angry*) I didn't think it would be like this. Bein' my age. *My age!* Bein' older doesn't bear thinkin' about . . . Should be us who's on the fuckin' bonfire . . .

UPSIDE DOWN: It'd be all right if we had y'know like a girlfriend. To go out with. To do things with.

UPRIGHT: Yeah . . . *yeah*. To be some rich woman's toy boy, that's one of my biggest ambitions, that is. I'd let her buy me all new clothes. From Next. Fuck Top Shop, and the catalogue. And I'd be sat there beside her in the back of her chauffeur-driven black BMW with a crate of ale in the boot on our way home from . . . somewhere. Like a restaurant . . . I'm not ugly. Am I?

UPSIDE DOWN: Nah. Not really . . . not at all.

UPRIGHT: Y'd think I was. I wouldn't be ugly if I had money.

UPSIDE DOWN: Nobody would.

UPRIGHT: Where d'y'think rich women hang out?

UPSIDE DOWN: . . . Is this a trick question?

UPRIGHT: No. I wanna know.

UPSIDE DOWN: I dunno. Stables? Health Farms. Places like that. Wine bars. Dress shops.

UPRIGHT: (*Nods*) It's worth thinking about . . .

UPSIDE DOWN: Er . . . yeah . . .

(UPSIDE DOWN *looks at* UPRIGHT *in bewilderment. Then they both stare out. As they do so, see a door open in a flat on the next-to-top floor of the building. A light comes on in the room. See* MAL, *a woman in her thirties. Attractive, speeding, wearing jeans and a raincoat.* MAL *slams the door and locks it. She races to the big window. Opens and looks out.*)

MAL: Oh God! Oh God! (MAL *grabs the phone on the toy box and dials. A good attempt at 'calmness':*) . . . Mother, mother, it's me, would you . . . no, it's not raining – not here, no – *yes*, I'm certain. Mother, would you keep the kids with you a . . . Mother, he *wants* to be a vegetarian, it's nothing to do with me, blame *Blue Peter* . . . yes, yes, but I'll be there as soon as I can. Really, I've got to go. (MAL *slams the phone down. Shouts with exasperation as she dials again.*) Martin, Martin, *I'm sorry* – I'm sorry to phone you at home, but you've got to come to The Heights now . . . *Martin*, I need you. And I'm in trouble . . . *Please*.

(MAL *puts the phone down and begins a frenzy of action. Principally filling a suitcase with the first clothes – hers and the children's – that come to hand. Whereupon we see* MAL *go to the large, framed poster on the wall facing the window.* MAL *takes it off the wall. Reveals a small wall safe. Flicks the combination lock. Opens the safe. As fierce banging on her flat door begins.* MAL *panics. Begins to grab plastic bags of fifty-pound notes out of the safe. Deposits them in a Tesco bag feverishly.* MAL *finally takes a set of documents out of the safe and puts them in the bag. Closes the safe, replaces the framed poster. At a hurried tilt. As the banging continues. Until the banging stops. See* MAL *hesitate. Listens. Goes to pick up her suitcase.*)

FIRST BRUTE: (*Outside*) Coming!

6

SECOND BRUTE: (*Outside*) Ready or not!
    (*Hear the first sounds of a sledgehammer to the door.* MAL *yelps.*
    Discards her suitcase. Runs to the light switch. Turns the lights
    off. Another crash of hammers. MAL *runs to the large window.*
    She pushes window open. The phone rings at her side. She jumps
    and screams. Hesitates. Picks up the phone.)
MAL: *Yes!* . . . Mother, mother . . . no, no, y'can put mustard on
    his veggie burgers – there is no meat in mustard, mother . . .
    yes, I'm sure – (*Another crash of hammers.*) – I've go to go
    now, mother – there's someone at the door. (MAL *throws the*
    phone down. Hesitates at the open window. Another crash
    against the door. MAL *steps out on to the ledge, holding her Tesco*
    bag. Puts the bag over her arm, edges past the window and then
    half turns and pushes it shut. Looks down. Almost silently:)
    Aaaaaaaaaaaaagggggggggghhhh! (MAL *turns back towards the*
    window. Another loud crash is heard.) . . . This is . . . this is a
    strange way to go to the shops . . . (*She edges, back turned to*
    the drop, away from the window. Towards the centre stage. MAL
    knocks on the window of the flat in darkness next to hers.) Mr
    McKenzie, Mr – (*Mumbles.*) Oh fuckin' hell, he died in
    September . . .
    (*And the door to her flat is broken down. Perhaps in the light*
    from the back corridor, see two men in overcoats maraud into the
    room with sledgehammers. They reach the window as another
    man enters the room. He flicks the light switch on.)
FIRST BRUTE: . . . She's . . . she's not here.
    (*Both* BRUTES *still look. See the other man,* SHAUN BARRY, *as*
    he moves into the body of the room. He too is in his late thirties,
    expensively dressed. His classless accent will give way at times,
    notably in anger, to reveal his Liverpool origins.)
SHAUN: I don't believe it.
    (*He looks around the room. Looks anxiously towards the tilted*
    framed poster. Then towards his two BRUTES. *Hesitates. Turns*
    away. Rapidly levels up the framed poster. Walks away towards
    the window and looks down. MAL *scurries further away as the*
    window opens.)
FIRST BRUTE: She's got to be in these flats somewhere. Sammy
    saw her come in.

SECOND BRUTE: Is right.

SHAUN: *So find her.* (*As* SHAUN *focuses on distant sights. Puzzled. Turns towards the door.*) Hang on a minute, come and have a look at this!

(SHAUN *waits for the* BRUTES *to trudge back.* SHAUN *points out of the window.*)

Look at that! There's fires going up everywhere!

FIRST BRUTE: . . . It's, er, Guy Fawkes Night, Boss.

SHAUN: Oh yeah. Yeah. Well go ahead, find her.

SECOND BRUTE: Is right.

(*The* BRUTES *leave the flat.* SHAUN *goes to the safe, sees it is empty, bangs the safe shut.*)

SHAUN: No, no, bitch!

(SHAUN *storms out of the room. See a man in his early forties edge out on to the sixth-floor ledge from stage right. He is carrying a briefcase. Moves his free hand uneasily towards his trouser zip.*)

MAN ON LEDGE: (*Mumbling*) 'Excuse me, can I use your toilet please?' 'No, piss off. Use the corridor like everyone else . . .'

MAL: (*Ducking down*) *Oh no!*

UPSIDE DOWN: Did . . . did you hear someone then?

UPRIGHT: Nah. But that bastard body builder collapsed one of my ear drums as well.

UPSIDE DOWN: Didn't do much buildin' with your body, did he?

MAN ON LEDGE: I can't take any more!

UPRIGHT: Neither can I . . . *Who the fuck's that?*

MAN ON LEDGE: *I just can't!*

UPSIDE DOWN: Fuckin' hell – there's someone down there.

(*They both lean over further to look. Come back.*)

MAN ON LEDGE: I wanna die!

UPRIGHT: Let's spit on him!

UPSIDE DOWN: Yeah, that'll fuckin' kill him.

(*The two boys lean over to spit. As the two* BRUTES, *still with sledgehammers, approach.*)

FIRST BRUTE: *Hey you – you two!*

UPSIDE DOWN: *It wasn't us!*

UPRIGHT: *We didn't do it!*

(UPSIDE DOWN *looks down at his paint-splattered hands with*

8

unbridled horror. Both lads turn around. UPSIDE DOWN
*contrives to put his hands behind his back. He attempts to hide
them up the cuffs of his coat.)*

UPSIDE DOWN: Honest. I'm allergic to paint.

UPRIGHT: An' . . . an' . . . an' I've got weak wrists!
  (*The two* BRUTES *approach. They tower over the boys. The boys
  look up, plaintively.*)

UPSIDE DOWN: You're not sort of one of them vigilantes, are y'?
  Like?

UPRIGHT: Or a body builder, by any chance?

FIRST BRUTE: Shut up, dickhead.

UPRIGHT: Certainly, sir.

FIRST BRUTE: You seen anyone up here?

UPRIGHT: Yeah, two other lads with, er, aerosols.

UPSIDE DOWN: Shoutin' 'Anarchy!' An' that.

UPRIGHT: 'Fuck things up!'

UPSIDE DOWN: 'On purpose!' An' . . . an' . . . 'Break the rules!'

UPRIGHT: Er, 'Feed the poor!'

UPSIDE DOWN: An' 'Eat the rich!'
  (*Both lads wince. The* BRUTES *exchange puzzled looks.*)

UPRIGHT: . . . Or somethin'.

UPSIDE DOWN: 'Power to the people!'
  (*He raises his fist in salute. Realizes it is covered in paint. Hauls
  it down with his other hand.*)

UPRIGHT: 'Up the revolution!'

FIRST BRUTE: And 'Come on you Blues'?

UPRIGHT: Yeah! Er no, I dunno. I'm a bit deaf.

FIRST BRUTE: A woman.

SECOND BRUTE: Up here.

UPSIDE DOWN: No, there's no one else here.

UPRIGHT: Now those two other lads have gone.

MAN ON LEDGE: I WANNA DIE!

UPRIGHT: Apart from him, that is.

UPSIDE DOWN: But he isn't a woman.

MAN ON LEDGE: I WANNA DIE! BUT I WANNA PUSH!
  (*Both* BRUTES *look down over the railings.*)

FIRST BRUTE: It's only a bloke.

UPRIGHT: I know. Shall we spit on him?

9

SECOND BRUTE: Yeah, all right.

FIRST BRUTE: Oh f'Christ's sake, Tommy, y'forty fuckin' four.

SECOND BRUTE: (*Hopefully*) But young at heart. (*Twirls prettily.*)

FIRST BRUTE: Come 'head. (*To lads.*) A woman.

SECOND BRUTE: Is right. A woman.

> (*The lads stare blankly at the two* BRUTES.)

FIRST BRUTE: Y'do know what a woman is, don't y'?

UPRIGHT: (*Aggrieved*) Course I do – I've been to Butlins.

FIRST BRUTE: This particular one's in her thirties, jeans, raincoat,
fit. And there'll be a few quid in it for you if you find her . . .

> (FIRST BRUTE *moves away.*)

SECOND BRUTE: (*Pointing down*) But what about him?

FIRST BRUTE: Oh, spit on him if you want to, but hurry up.

SECOND BRUTE: No y'know, he might jump.

FIRST BRUTE: We'll move the car.

UPSIDE DOWN: You're, er, in y'car then, are y'?

FIRST BRUTE: No, we couldn't get it up the stairs. Come on.

UPSIDE DOWN: What make is it? Like?

> (FIRST BRUTE *turns back to them.*)

FIRST BRUTE: A red Cortina.

UPRIGHT: (*Turning away*, sotto voce) It's not any more.

FIRST BRUTE: And I'll take your fuckin' hands off at the armpits if
you so much as lay one finger on it. Understand?

UPRIGHT: Last thing on our minds.

UPSIDE DOWN: Sir.

FIRST BRUTE: It will be, believe me.

> (*The* BRUTES *depart.* UPSIDE DOWN *climbs over the railings to
look down.*)

UPRIGHT: Don't bother. Y'might not want to come back.

UPSIDE DOWN: . . . . Oh fuck . . .

UPRIGHT: Worse than fuck. There should be another word worse
than fuck.

MAN ON LEDGE: (*With quiet disgust*) Ohhh!

> (*As* UPSIDE DOWN *stares at his paint-spattered hands*, UPRIGHT
looks down.)

UPRIGHT: Wanna form a trio, pal?

UPSIDE DOWN: I'll have to get this paint off me hands. And then
we'll have to hide.

UPRIGHT: It's not like the Infants School when you were a kid, you know. 'Got y', one two three!' It'll be 'Come here, twat features, stand there, take that – smack smack, blood and snot and another bastard oxygen tent.' *And I am not going to be beaten to buggery ever again. I've fuckin' had enough! I've had fuckin' enough! Enough I have fuckin' had!*

UPSIDE DOWN: . . . Are you tryin' to tell me somethin', Jimmy?

UPRIGHT: IS THIS ALL THERE FUCKIN' IS? Fuckin' hell, I think I'm dyin' by instalments. (*He slumps over the railings. To* MAN ON LEDGE.) I'll beat you to the bottom, pal.

UPSIDE DOWN: (*Puts his arm around* UPRIGHT) Look, we'll find somewhere. Might even find that woman for them.

UPRIGHT: . . . Any woman'd do me. I haven't really been to Butlins. (*Looks to the* MAN ON LEDGE.) Wouldn't half like to see him jump, though.

UPSIDE DOWN: So would I.

UPRIGHT: Please me no end, that would. Knowin' someone else was . . . in a worse state than me.

UPSIDE DOWN: (*Shouts down*) Don't do it, mate – don't jump! Not yet, anyway. Come 'head.
(*Grabs hold of* UPRIGHT *and they begin to move away and off the roof.*)

MAN ON LEDGE: (*Mumbling*) Huh, huh-huh, huh-huh-huh. Jump . . . jump to it.
(*He peeks down, leans back apprehensively. As he does so, see* MAL *come back around the building, having done a circuit. She looks into her flat in passing, tries the window. Moves on towards the centre. Listens.*)

MAN ON LEDGE: . . . Certain death. (*Shrugs. Slight laugh.*) Death is certain. That was made very clear to me a long time ago. Every Ash Wednesday. Ashes to ashes. Dust to dust. Wall to wall. (*Giggles.*) Toe to toe. Inch by inch. Heart to heart. Head to foot. Hand to mouth. Mouth to mouth. From here to . . . eternity . . . Indeed, indeed. Do the deed. *Come on. Come on.*
(*As the* MAN ON LEDGE *builds in his intensity,* MAL *is caught between being caught or going to the rescue. And the two* BRUTES *with sledgehammers return to the roof.*)

SECOND BRUTE: This sledgehammer's makin' my arm hurt, you know.

FIRST BRUTE: Use your other hand.

SECOND BRUTE: I've thought of that, but then both my arms 'd hurt . . .

(*As they approach the railings, hear a phone ring. Both* BRUTES *drop their sledgehammers and take out their portable phones simultaneously. The* SECOND BRUTE *seems puzzled.*)

BOTH BRUTES: Hello . . .

FIRST BRUTE: . . . No, she's not on the roof, boss.

SECOND BRUTE: (*Looking at his phone*) I can't hear anyone.

FIRST BRUTE: (*Withering him*) And I don't think she's visiting neighbours, because she's hardly got any. Almost everywhere's all boarded up.

SECOND BRUTE: Oh aye, yeah. (*Puts his phone away.*)

FIRST BRUTE: . . . Right, boss. (*Puts his phone away, looks to the* SECOND BRUTE, *mimics him:*) 'I can't hear anyone . . .' The boss's on his way up . . .

(*The two* BRUTES *move away from the railings to welcome* SHAUN *upon his arrival on the roof. As* MAL *climbs the drainpipe, her head appears over the Man on Ledge's ledge. He recoils with surprise.*)

MAL: Two things . . . right? Don't kill yourself – and please, for God's sake, be quiet . . . good, that's very quiet.

MAN ON LEDGE: . . . Don't kill myself?

MAL: Just as important as being quiet.

MAN ON LEDGE: Imagine I'm black and I'm also a kettle.

MAL: Pardon?

MAN ON LEDGE: You're a pot.

(*As* SHAUN *enters, walking across the roof with his* BRUTES *in attendance, a couple of respectful steps behind.*)

MAL: . . . No no, I'm not trying to kill myself – I'm out here to stay alive!

MAN ON LEDGE: (*Flatly*) You must live very dangerously.

(SHAUN *approaches the railings.*)

SHAUN: . . . This is serious.

FIRST BRUTE: I know.

(*The* BRUTES *join* SHAUN *at the railings.*)

SHAUN: You don't.

FIRST BRUTE: I know.

SECOND BRUTE: Is right.

(SHAUN *turns his head and looks coldly at him*.)

An' I don't know neither.

FIRST BRUTE: I only said 'I know' because it was sort of expected
of me.

SHAUN: I know. *But you don't know – you never know – why do you
always say you know when you don't know – when all you know
is nothing?* Hey? Hey? ANSWER ME!

FIRST BRUTE: I . . . I can't, Boss, because all I can think of to say
is . . .

SHAUN: I know. And God knows, you don't know how lucky you
are.

FIRST BRUTE: I know. (*Closes his eyes*.)

SHAUN: Where were you, hey, where were you before I came
along? Come on, answer me that!

FIRST BRUTE: I was head bouncer at the Fix Me Up A Go Go
Club, Boss.

SECOND BRUTE: And I was a dance teacher.

(*The others look at him. He deepens his voice*.)

Well, I was.

SHAUN: (*Sated, looking away, facing out*) So there we have it – and
don't you forget it . . .

(*Hear the alarm bells of a fire engine approaching from a
distance*. SHAUN *can follow it through the estate*.)

. . . But what did I do? What did I do to her? *What did I do
wrong?*

FIRST BRUTE: . . . I *don't* know.

SECOND BRUTE: And neither do I.

SHAUN: . . . Hang on, that fire engine's coming here.

SECOND BRUTE: It'll be that feller on the ledge.

SHAUN: *What?*

SECOND BRUTE: Yeah, there's some feller down there threatenin'
to jump.

(SHAUN *tries to look directly down*. MAL *tries to shrivel behind a
drainpipe*.)

Why do they always pick on these flats?

FIRST BRUTE: Concrete surrounds. They mean it when they go off here. No going back for seconds with a slight limp, oh no . . . Someone's bound to phone the papers.

SECOND BRUTE: The cameras came last time, remember?

SHAUN: Oh no.

FIRST BRUTE: Oh aye, yeah – there was this lad with a motorbike – built a fuckin' big ramp right here – (*Points down.*) an' then tried to make the roof on the next block of flats. (*He points out.*)

SECOND BRUTE: Rang all the papers first – the telly an' all that – local radio – there were people with picnics an' everythin'.

FIRST BRUTE: Gave it his best shot though, didn't he?

SECOND BRUTE: Oh aye, yeah. Gorra admire him for that.

SHAUN: (*Whispers*) I can't be seen here.

FIRST BRUTE: (*Shudders as he points out again*) – Went straight through that window over there – landed on a couple watchin' *Blind Date*.

SECOND BRUTE: Serves them fuckin' well right.

SHAUN: (*Shakes his head*) I can't be seen here . . . I can't be seen here – here in this shithole . . . spent twenty years of my life hiding and disguising the fact that I was born and brought up here – here in this fucking shithole.

FIRST BRUTE: Er, er, parts of it are all right, y'know.
(SHAUN *turns and stares at him.*)
Er, like the parks an' that, an', er, the river, it's er . . . a lot cleaner than it used to be.

SECOND BRUTE: An' have y'seen the Albert Docks, Boss, that's –

SHAUN: Of course I've fucking seen the Albert Docks, Boss – I helped to rebuild the Albert Docks!

SECOND BRUTE: Did you?

SHAUN: Came up here after the riots in '81 with Michael . . . (*Looks at them.*) Heseltine. Remember that big, blue executive bus of his that drove us all around – the leading lights – industrialists and bankers and men of . . . property – I was on that bus – me and Michael – we had dinner together later – he was shocked – and I was pretending I was from Buckinghamshire and pretending I was shocked as well . . . by the state of this run-down fucking shithole.

14

FIRST BRUTE: . . . So, er, y'know, er, how come like, if you, er, hated it up here so much, you, er, met her up here, y'know, this one – the, er, whatsits – the skirt?

SHAUN: . . . I came home – *back* – I came back for a funeral . . . (*Thinks*.) It was . . . my mother's . . . I think.
(*The two* BRUTES *look at each other behind* SHAUN's *back, genuinely horrified and disgusted*.)
Yeah, my mother's. Met her then. In a club in town . . . and now she could be my fuckin' funeral. I knew, I knew when I phoned her at work – work! What kind of work's involved in social services – but I knew then – I could tell – took too much to heart the things I'd left her – only business, I said – I warned her – I'll do the business, you give me the pleasure. I was good to that woman. And what's more I was about to take her out of this fuckin', fuckin' . . .

FIRST BRUTE: *Shithole!*

SHAUN: I was gonna give her a better life. (*Thumps railings*.) I was good to that woman!

SECOND BRUTE: Is right. You were very kind to her.

FIRST BRUTE: You gave her lots of valuable things.

SHAUN: Yeh! Too many as it turns out. *And I can't be seen here!*

FIRST BRUTE: Why don't you go downstairs? And then Sammy can cover outside.

SECOND BRUTE: Is right.

FIRST BRUTE: Even better, I'll move me car around the back, and then you can go and sit in it, if y'want. I've got the latest Pavarotti in there – an', er, some Picketty Witch.

SECOND BRUTE: Don't worry, we'll find her.

SHAUN: . . . What about the door downstairs?

FIRST BRUTE: Me brother works for the Council. I'll get him to send a carpenter out.

SHAUN: From . . . from the Council?

FIRST BRUTE: Yeah. Should only take a fortnight.
(*Both* BRUTES *laugh*.)
No, they have improved recently . . .

SHAUN: . . . There's money in this for you, boys. Big money. More money than you've ever seen before. But, as you might expect, it's payment by results.

MAN ON LEDGE: Oh listen to that, payment by results.
SHAUN: (*Quietly, matter of fact*) Just shut up and jump.
   (SHAUN *and the* BRUTES *depart.* MAL *looks up towards the railings. Listens.*)
MAL: I don't want the money, Shaun Barry. You can have the stinking money . . . (*She looks towards the Tesco bag.*) . . . I'll just open this can of worms . . . (*She looks up towards the next ledge.*) They have gone, haven't they? . . . So, you don't have to be quiet any more – you did very well, no, you did, considering what you were hearing – but feel free, I'm all ears, I'm used to it – my job's to listen to other people's troubles. Their problems, their concerns, their heartaches, their worries, see if there's anything I can do to help – I'm an estate agent. (*She laughs. Alone.*) I'm not, I'm not. (*To herself.*) If I was, I'd have jumped long ago . . . Look – well, perhaps best not to look – listen – do you want to talk to me? Want me to talk to you . . . ? Prefer it if I talked to you, wouldn't you? I take it you're nodding your head there. My name's Mal. Mal . . . come on, a problem shared . . . huh? (*No answer. The* MAN ON LEDGE *stares out, huddled into himself.*)
Tell you what, I'm no judge of situations like this, but – and correct me if I'm wrong – but I bet you want cheering up – am I right or am I right? (*Still silence. To herself.*) Fucking hell . . . Well all right, this might cheer you up – working on the principle that other people's misfortunes cheer you up – you feel ashamed that they do – but they do – you just can't help yourself. It's true, isn't it . . . isn't it? (*No answer.*) He's probably a suicidal mime artist. (*She mimes him cutting his throat. Then shooting himself.*) Been dead for hours . . . But listen, this might cheer you up . . . I'm . . . I'm. . . well, judge for yourself – I've been married – once – and once was more than enough – once he left me for another woman and the mortgage was in arrears and the house was repossessed and I . . . (*She indicates her surroundings.*) returned from my adventures amongst the middle classes – mother of two children – by two different men – although not at the same time – I'm a democrat but not *that* liberal – however, one of

the men never knew he was a father because I never told him and he never asked before he went away. And the other man is married, and I am his other woman because although he is the father of my child, he is not, of course, married to me. Good hey? Wanna change places already . . . ? But so you see – here I am, only out here with you by accident, and I have made a considerable and almighty mess of my life, and you don't know the half. Because if you think that what you've heard so far is a disaster . . . well, my dear, those were the good times. For I also, for my sins, knew another man, recently of this roof, if not this parish, who, amongst his many gifts to me, has also given me the most . . . dirty and non-disposable linen. (MAL *looks at the plastic bag in her hand. Shudders.*) . . . But . . . but I still want to live! *Live!*

MAN ON LEDGE: Oh don't. Don't. You don't know.

MAL: Believe me, you're not –

MAN ON LEDGE: Mad?

MAL: It's unlikely.

MAN ON LEDGE: I am, I am, I couldn't be here if I wasn't, don't take that away from me, I have to be mad, I want to be mad, I am mad.

MAL: *The world is mad!*

MAN ON LEDGE: I know that – and I have the proof here with me – (*Looks towards his briefcase.*) And that's the only thing that has kept me alive. Until now.

(MAL *begins to shin the drainpipe towards* MAN ON LEDGE. *He opens his briefcase, hesitates, then closes it. And* MOEY *arrives from below on the fireman's hoist.*)

MOEY: All right, all right, what the fuck's goin' on?

(MAL *returns to her ledge.*)

MAL: He's threatening to jump, but he isn't going to.

MOEY: And what's your game? Been to Tesco's for his Last Supper?

MAL: I was just passing by and –

MOEY: Yeah, course you were – but all I know is that we've had a report from a caring member of the community – perhaps *the* caring member of this community – that there were two people up here – that's you and him as far as I can see – so come ahead, don't mess me around, it's Guy Fawkes Night, I haven't got the time – I've got to go and get stoned to death in a minute. Are you gettin' in or what?

MAL: What about him?

MOEY: Ladies first. The age of chivalry is not yet dead, y'stupid bitch. In. In. Come on. I have a stoning to go to.

MAL: I am, I am. (*Gets in.*) Have you ever tried charm?
(MOEY *begins to move the hoist up.*)

MOEY: Don't be daft, I deal with the public. (*Looks up.*) Right. Are you two related in any way other than a love of high places and a desire to die?

MAL: No, I have never seen him before in my life.

MOEY: (*To* MAN ON LEDGE) OK. Room for one more inside. Move along the bus now. Been waiting long, pal?

MAN ON LEDGE: Go away.

MOEY: Look, are you gettin' in or what?

MAN ON LEDGE: No.

MOEY: I can take one more.

MAN ON LEDGE: I can't take any more.

MOEY: You full up as well, are'y? I know the feelin', but don't worry about it – the mood passes. Come on, soft girl here got on. You can do it too.

MAN ON LEDGE: Leave me alone.

MAL: Let me talk to him. (*To* MAN ON LEDGE.) Listen to me, whoever you are –

MOEY: Do me a favour. Leave it to a professional. (*To* MAN ON LEDGE.) Come on, this is y'last chance, bollocks, and I'm tellin' you now, half-way down, y'll change y'fuckin' mind, most of them do – and then it'll be too fuckin' late. (*Pause.*) Fine. I tried me best.

MAL: That's your best?

MOEY: Under the circumstances – yes. Let's go.
(*They start to move down.*)

MAL: He needs help.

MOEY: He'll need a shovel the way he's going on.

MAL: (*Looking up*) Stay there. I'll get help. I'll go down and get help!

MOEY: I wouldn't bother – that lot down there can't even help

themselves – except to other people's property. From the
cradle to the gaol, that's this fuckin' estate. The bastards
only go to the shops when they're shut.

(MAL *looks down. Focuses. Panics.*)

MAL: I CAN'T GO DOWN THERE!

MOEY: Behave.

MAL: Put me back up. PUT ME BACK UP!

MOEY: That's goin' to look good at my tribunal, isn't it? 'I
returned the lady to the ledge, sir, whereupon some seconds
later, she passed me at a speed approaching eighty-five miles
an hour.'

MAL: I can't go down there – there's someone down there I don't
want to see.

MOEY: Look, I'm not fuckin' well responsible for your social
diary, madam.

(MAL *climbs out of the hydraulic platform. Clings to the hoist
with her hands and feet.*)

MAL: I'll jump, I'll jump!

MOEY: Oh . . . oh! All right. (*He stops the platform. And then begins
to move upwards towards the railings on the roof.*) 'Be a fireman,
my son.' 'D'y' reckon, Dad?' 'Yes, my son, do something
worthwhile and honourable with your life, save other
people's lives . . .' Wish you were dead.

MAL: (*Shouting down*) You can have your money, Shaun, you can
have it! I was going to do some good with it! Good! But you
can have it – I don't want it!

MOEY: And which one of the gatherin' fuckin' multitude are you
talking to now?

MAL: Just put me on the roof.

MOEY: (*Pushing back fireman's helmet, tugging forelock*) 'Yes,
ma'am, that'll be two and sixpence, not counting gratuities . . .'

MAL: (*To* MAN ON LEDGE *in passing*) I'll be back.

MOEY: Don't encourage him. If I thought you were coming back
for me, I'd fuckin' jump. (*To* MAN ON LEDGE) I may never
pass this way again, pal.

(*The hydraulic platform goes above the railings on the roof.* MAL
*climbs from the platform edge and runs across the roof and down
the stairs. However, as soon as* MOEY *has finished his previous*

speech, we see UPRIGHT *and* UPSIDE DOWN *passing Mal's flat. Or perhaps we see them entering Mal's flat, having been lured in by the door off the hinges and the prospects of a washbasin.*)

MAN ON LEDGE: I don't care.

MOEY: I can wait. I'll wait. Smoke?

(*The boys are naturally nervous and circumspect.* UPSIDE DOWN *goes to the window and opens it. Looks down.*)

UPSIDE DOWN: The car's gone.

UPRIGHT: Yeah, I know, and it's all a dream and we'll wake up in the morning alongside Madonna, and she'll say 'Fuck being a virgin, boys, I'm all yours.' Come ahead.

UPSIDE DOWN: (*Turning and observing*) But there's a telly. And a stereo.

UPRIGHT: Aren't we in enough trouble? Let's just scrub our hands and fuck off.

UPSIDE DOWN: (*Pointing*) Thomas the Tank Engine.

UPRIGHT: It probably belongs to a retarded muscle-man. (*He talks like an idiot as they move out of sight.*) 'You got my tank engine? You got Thomas? You wanna be a Woodentop?' (*They go into the body of the flat to wash their hands. Meanwhile,* MOEY *is descending in the fireman's hoist.*)

MOEY: Look at it this way, pal, no, really we all have bad times in our lives, come on, you know that, and listen, however sad you might be right now just remember this –

MAN ON LEDGE: Leave me alone, I'm happy.

MOEY: And I'm fuckin' Grumpy! Well, fuck you then – fuck off, go on, fuck off and jump. Go ahead. I've got priorities, pal, I've got property to look after – if you're going to take life personal, if y'want y'ankles around y'shoulder blades an' y'knee caps for earrings, go ahead and jump, get it over with, but strawberry jam on the fuckin' pavement is no fuckin' answer at all and is going to make no fuckin' difference!

(MOEY *descends as he speaks, and is almost out of sight as he finishes.*)

MAN ON LEDGE: (*Wearily*) There's no need to use such bad language.

MOEY: Oh fuck off.

(*And off. As* MAL *hurls into her flat. Goes to her window to open*

20

it. Double-takes as she realizes the window is open. Looks out of the window.)

MAL: Ohhhhhhhhhhhhhh . . .

(MAL *turns towards the far wall. Pulls the framed poster off the wall. Hurls it away. Finds the combination for the safe. Opens the safe. As* UPRIGHT *and* UPSIDE DOWN *come into sight in the flat. They stand and watch her, bewildered. While* MAL *begins to take out of her bag the plastic bags of serious money and hurl them at the safe. Some fall on the floor.* UPRIGHT *and* UPSIDE DOWN *stop being bewildered. Become excited.* MAL *hurls the last bag of money at the safe. She runs to the doorway. The phone rings.* MAL *hesitates. See* SHAUN *on the roof holding his portable phone to his ear.* MAL *reluctantly goes to phone. Picks it up. Listens.*)

SHAUN: Oh, you're home. (*Tuts.*) Sorry about the door. *Don't hang up.* Listen to me, listen to me! *Please!* Listen to me. (*Pause. She doesn't hang up.*)

Mal, remember the good times. Remember Paris? Remember Rome? 'Three Coins in the Fountain' – Remember Acapulco? *Don't hang up!* . . . I'm in trouble, Mal, help me, please help me – look, look, let's sleep on it – let's sleep on it together – we'll go away – where d'y'wanna go – who d'y'wanna go with us – you wanna take your children? – you wanna take your mother? DON'T HANG UP! Mal – *Mal*, I'm in trouble, help me, kid, please help me – don't let them hurt me – I know you – you'll never let anyone hurt me.

(MAL *puts the phone down. Runs out of the flat.*)

OK Mal, it's shit, baby, swim in it.

(SHAUN *leaves the roof. The two boys in the flat come out of hiding.*)

UPSIDE DOWN: (*Pointing*) . . . M . . . m . . . money!

UPRIGHT: Lots of money!

UPSIDE DOWN: Fuckin' thousands and thousands!

UPRIGHT: It . . .

UPSIDE DOWN: Yeh!

UPRIGHT: It . . .

UPSIDE DOWN: Yeh!

UPRIGHT: It . . .

UPSIDE DOWN: Yeh!

UPRIGHT: It must be Ken Dodd's flat!

UPSIDE DOWN: (*Sings*) Happiness, happiness, the greatest gift . . .

UPRIGHT: Nah, he hid his money under the floorboards.

UPSIDE DOWN: I'm – we're both –

UPRIGHT: Yeh!

UPSIDE DOWN: Both –

UPRIGHT: Yeh!

UPSIDE DOWN: Both –

UPRIGHT: Yeh!

UPSIDE DOWN: Scared.

UPRIGHT: I'm fuckin' terrified – but fuck it!

(UPRIGHT *races back towards the wall.* UPSIDE DOWN *joins him.* UPRIGHT *begins to pull the money bags out of the safe.* UPRIGHT *begins to scoop them off the floor. Whereupon . . . they hear the* FIRST BRUTE *shout from a distance.*)

FIRST BRUTE: Hey – hey you, girl!

SECOND BRUTE: Yeah you – come here!

(UPSIDE DOWN *and* UPRIGHT *madly push the money back into the safe. Close but do not lock the safe. They hurl the framed poster back on to the wall and hide in the toilet. The* BRUTES *enter the room.*)

FIRST BRUTE: (*Out of window*) Come on, love, let's get this over with. I want you in here now.

SECOND BRUTE: Is right.

(*The boys try to escape.* UPRIGHT *knocks down Mal's suitcase as he leaves.*)

FIRST BRUTE: But I want you two even fuckin' more.

(*The boys depart towards the roof. Shortly to be followed by the two* BRUTES. *Panting. Meanwhile,* MAL, *having recovered her breath, is moving away, stage right, in search of an open window and rescue.*)

MAL: (*Shouting up*) Are you still there?

MAN ON LEDGE: (*Flatly*) No. I'm out. Out of my mind. This is a recorded message . . .

(MAL *goes.*)

. . . Come on, *come on!*
(*And the two lads burst on to the roof. Go desperately towards the railings. And the two* BRUTES *appear on the roof, without breath. The* FIRST BRUTE *reveals a paint-stained hand.*)

FIRST BRUTE: My car, boys. My car's bleedin' an' it's bruised.

UPRIGHT: (*Childlike*) Ahhh, poor little Cortina, kiss it better.

UPSIDE DOWN: D'you want a requiem mass, Jimmy?

FIRST BRUTE: My car –

SECOND BRUTE: What . . . what about the boss's woman?

FIRST BRUTE: She's not goin' nowhere.
(*The* BRUTES *take a pace towards the lads. They begin to skirt each other, but there is the obstacle of the railings.*)
But my car. My precious car. It's got a head wound. A dented head. Just like what you're going to have.

UPSIDE DOWN: We . . . we can offer you money.

UPRIGHT: Sir.

UPSIDE DOWN: Kind sir.

UPRIGHT: We know where there's lots of money.

UPSIDE DOWN: Big money!

UPRIGHT: Tall . . . er, money.

FIRST BRUTE: No money in the world can compensate for the damage done to a '68 Mark Two Ford Cortina with drop-chassis overdrive and delayed-action camshaft acceleration.

UPRIGHT: Listen, pal –

FIRST BRUTE: Shut up and stand up straight, and take your medicine like a man. I loved that car. Every Sunday I worshipped and washed and leathered it. I made that car gleam in the dark. It was like a shrine to me. It was the brother I never had, that car.

UPRIGHT: (*Carefully considers the last speech*) . . . He's fuckin' mental.

UPSIDE DOWN: I know. Let's go.
(*The boys try to escape.* UPSIDE DOWN *goes over the railings.*)

FIRST BRUTE: (*Frothing*) Hey – hey, you two walkin' fuckin' funerals – the only place you're going is eternal fuckin' hell – do not stop – with a personal escort to the very gates from me! (*He thumps himself in the chest.*) From me – from yours truly! An' – an' what's more – when I have finished with yis –

I won't have finished with yis cos don't think y'funerals'll be
the finish of it – oh no – oh no – it'll only be the beginning!

UPRIGHT: (*Looking down, from the edge of the ledge*)
Aaaaaaaaaagggggggggghhhh! Aaaaaagggggghhhh! What am I
doing here? I'm gonna die – I'm gonna die – just when I was
nearly rich!

(UPSIDE DOWN *goes past the* MAN ON LEDGE.)

UPSIDE DOWN: Climb down!

UPRIGHT: Fuck that! I wanna get back on the roof! I wanna be
beaten up! Let me back! I have one ear drum left – you can
have it!

(*The* BRUTES *laugh.*)

Fuckin' hell, fuckin' Cockneys in disguise! Cockneys from
Hell! (UPRIGHT, *in desperation, begins to climb down.*)

FIRST BRUTE: Yeah, but Hell's only the beginning, boys, cos,
y'know what, I'll be there visiting you in Southside cemetery
– I'll be there in the snow and the rain and the sun and the
mist of every passing season – I'll be there every single
sodding Sunday morning – until just before opening time at
the Cock and Bottle – but I'm not going to walk over y'graves
– oh no, not I – I'm not even going to dance on y'graves – no
no no – (*Claps hands.*) Even better than that – cos me and my
Cortina, boys, me and my Cortina're going to *drive* over
y'graves! – up and down and down and up and backwards
and forwards and forwards and backwards and on and on
and on and on and then, and then, only then will I be happy!
Oh, be still my beating heart.

(UPRIGHT *reaches the ledge on the fifth floor. He still has his
back turned, facing the wall. Gingerly turns around. Looks
about. Grabs tight hold of* UPSIDE DOWN. *Teetering gymnastics
occur. As* MAL *returns, from stage right, still trying to find an
open window and escape. And the two* BRUTES *see her.*)

FIRST BRUTE: Hey you, girl! Stay there. (*He goes.*)

UPRIGHT: (*Pointing, but not for long*) Hey you! This is all your
fault!

MAL: Why me?

UPRIGHT: I dunno – but it's not mine. What did I do? *What did I
do?*

UPSIDE DOWN: You held hold of my ankles while I was doing my painting.

UPRIGHT: Yeah you, y'bastard – it's all your fault!

(UPRIGHT *goes to let go of* UPSIDE DOWN *as if to hit him. Panics. Grabs hold of* UPSIDE DOWN *again. As the* FIRST BRUTE *enters the flat. Opens the window. Leans out, looks past the lads to* MAL.)

FIRST BRUTE: Hey!

UPRIGHT: (*To* FIRST BRUTE) We can be friends.

FIRST BRUTE: Get in here, girl. I want you in here now.

MAL: No! And I'm not your 'girl'.

UPRIGHT: I can be a girl! I can. I can be a Scottish girl!

MAL: I'm not coming back in.

UPRIGHT: (*High pitched and sort of Scottish*) I will. Oh och aye, Kenny Dalglish and a tam-o'-shanter! You can call me Aimi. Or Heather. Or Lulu.

FIRST BRUTE: All I'm going to call you is an ambulance. Afterwards. (*To* MAL.) It'll only get worse, you know. All this. The more attention you get, the worse it'll be. For you. (*The* FIRST BRUTE *slams the window shut, turns and goes out of the room, towards the roof.*)

UPRIGHT: Oh God, oh God. Oh hold me, Billy. Hold me.

UPSIDE DOWN: Not if you're a girl.

UPRIGHT: I'm not a girl.

(UPSIDE DOWN *holds* UPRIGHT *up.*)

UPSIDE DOWN: . . . I wish you were a girl.

UPRIGHT: Not now, Billy. Please. I've got a headache.

(*And* MOEY *returns. In the fireman's hoist.*)

MOEY: Oh hey, it's a fuckin' epidemic. And what's wrong with you two? Forced on to a YTS scheme, were y'? Giro not arrived? Pimples playin' y'up?

UPSIDE DOWN: Is this help or what?

UPRIGHT: It might be. Whatever it is, I'm gettin' off here.

FIRST BRUTE: (*From above*) Leave those two out there.

MOEY: Do I look like the fuckin' milkman?

FIRST BRUTE: They stay. Y'hear me?

MOEY: Listen, I've had enough threats today. You don't scare me – not in comparison to three hundred ten-year-olds at the

25

side of a wet bonfire.

FIRST BRUTE: We'll see about that.

MOEY: (*Easily*) Come over here and say that.

FIRST BRUTE: (*Pointing down*) You two get off there – we'll be waitin' for y' when y'land.

(*See* UPRIGHT *as he 'thinks'. And* MOEY *addresses the* MAN ON LEDGE.)

MOEY: Hey – hey! (*Whistles*.) Come fly with me – come here. (*To* MAL.) And I'll be coming back shortly for you, madam, I've never saved four at once before.

UPRIGHT: I think I might have thought of something, Billy.

MOEY: Come on, come on, be the first lucky customer?

UPRIGHT: I think it's a plan. Hey pal, we want to get off.

UPSIDE DOWN: What about them up there? What about all the . . . the whatsits. (*Sings*.) Happiness, happiness . . . (*Points to the flat*.)

UPRIGHT: I'm coming back to that. (*Winks again*.) That's a clue. (*Winks more*.) A clue.

FIRST BRUTE: You're not coming back at all – unless it's in another life, y'pair of little ball-bags.

MAN ON LEDGE: Huh, I just love the civilized manner in which we conduct our lives.

MOEY: And what kind of civilization d'you belong to – hey? One that thinks it's a good idea to do flyin' headers from a great fuckin' height?

UPRIGHT: Come on, Billy, I'm winkin' at y'.

UPSIDE DOWN: I know y'are – *but I don't know why!*

UPRIGHT: Trust me.

UPSIDE DOWN: Sound just like our Marie's boyfriend . . .

MOEY: (*To* MAL, *gently*) Come on, love.

MAL: I am not your love – and I cannot go down there.

(MOEY *swings the hoist slowly away*.)

UPRIGHT: Hey! Hey you two bouncer bastards – hey – you with the brother called Cortina!

UPSIDE DOWN: Oh no.

UPRIGHT: I'm gonna go down there now and knock fuck out of your Cortina, bollocks.

UPSIDE DOWN: *Jimmy!*

(UPSIDE DOWN *is slowly sinking out of sight in the platform with his hands over his eyes. As the platform begins to drop slowly.*)

UPRIGHT: I'm gonna kick its headlights in, I'm gonna smash its every window, I'm gonna rip its tyres apart, I'm gonna slash y'tiger fur upholstery, an' y'fluffy dice've had it too.

FIRST BRUTE: That's what you think – and I haven't got any fluffy dice! (*Reaches for his portable phone.*)

UPRIGHT: I bet you've got a plastic dog with big eyes in the back window though, y'wanker.

FIRST BRUTE: (*Into phone*) Sammy! Yeah – y'can see them? Good. Don't kill them till I get there. I'm looking forward to this, I haven't really hurt anyone for weeks . . .

(FIRST BRUTE *puts his phone away, grabs* SECOND BRUTE. *As* UPSIDE DOWN *whines in the hoist.*)

MAN ON LEDGE: Decency . . . honour . . . conscience.

MAL: (*Flatly*) Let me know when you're going – I'll come with you.

MAN ON LEDGE: Respect for others . . . manners, morality . . . values.

MAL: (*Laughs*) Values. Don't make me laugh.

MAN ON LEDGE: No laughing matter.

(MAL *stops laughing. Looks up.*)

MAL: (*Quietly*) Don't jump. Don't. You couldn't be in worse . . . muck than me. And I've got no intention of jumping.

(MAL *looks down. Starts laughing as she sees the hydraulic platform returning.* UPRIGHT *is behind* MOEY *and has hold of him around the neck.* UPSIDE DOWN *is on his knees, peeping out.*)

UPRIGHT: Faster! Faster!

MOEY: I can't go any fuckin' faster, do I look like Nigel Mansell?

UPSIDE DOWN: But what is this, Jimmy?

UPRIGHT: It's me plan. It's me get-rich plan. It's like the fuckin' turning point in our lives, Billy, it's that moment like when that apple fell on the feller's head in the bath and he shouted 'Eureka'! It's like fog clearin'. It's like 'Blue skies, nothing but blue skies' . . .

UPSIDE DOWN: I still don't get it.

UPRIGHT: (*To* UPSIDE DOWN) Listen, they're down there, right?

We're up here. Just below us is the rich bit of the get-rich plan. Fuckin' brilliant, hey? Fuckin' superb. Fuckin' brains or what? *I* thought of that. *Me!*

UPSIDE DOWN: But what happens when they come back up again?

(UPRIGHT *considers briefly.* UPRIGHT *then goes into panic as he contemplates more brain damage.*)

UPRIGHT: I never thought of that bit. But I don't care. I won't care once I'm rich. I'll buy that bastard a new car. And if that doesn't work, I'll go private and get new teeth, a nose job and a deaf aid. But I don't care! I wanna be rich! Jump.

UPSIDE DOWN: Which way?

UPRIGHT: I'm not a violent person usually. Jump.

(*They both jump.* UPRIGHT *runs off, singing 'Money'.* UPSIDE DOWN *follows him.*)

MOEY: OVENS! Big ovens, fuckin' big ovens, doors always open, fuckin' big fires blazin' out – that's what I'd have – any time of the day or night – throw the bastards in – dickheads like them – drug pushers, granny bashers, muggers, murderers, rapists, perverts, pricks with Porsches, estate agents, Spanish time-share salesmen, members of the Monday Club, urban fuckin' terrorists, half of Northern Ireland, all the Arab states, people in possession of a Pink Floyd album, any fuckin' album'll do – anyone above the rank of lance corporal in the army – muck rakers, dog owners, stone throwers, fire makers, the whole fuckin' cast of *Prisoner of Cell Block H*, the total white population of Australia, South Africa, the Isle of Man and Bognor Regis, the feller next door but one with the drum kit *and* the thievin' twat across the road; Bernard Manning and James Whale; Bob Monkhouse and Tony fuckin' Blackburn; John fuckin' Mcfuckin' Cririck; that fuckin' twat Lamont, Major fuckin' Minor, the fuckin' lot – get in there – go on, off to fuck!

MAL: That's hardly Christian, is it?

MOEY: CHRISTIANS! I fuckin' forgot Christians! Go on, burn y'bastards!

(*As* UPSIDE DOWN *and* UPRIGHT *crash into Mal's flat. They*

tear down the framed poster, grab open the safe. Exultant. Grab
the money. Then tear-arse out again, stuffing the money into their
trouser pockets. And go the way that the two Brutes went. While
MOEY *passes* MAL *as he descends the hoist.*)

MAL: . . . And all that would be left when the fires had burnt
would be good, decent people?

MOEY: Yeah.

MAL: And fucking fascists like you with your fucking ovens!
(MOEY *shrugs as he goes down in the hoist and off.*)

MAN ON LEDGE: Do you . . . have to? Do you *really* have to?

MAL: . . . Have to what?

MAN ON LEDGE: Language. Language . . . language is supposed
to communicate. What kind of communication is . . . is
'f'ing' this and 'f'ing' that – 'f' this and 'f' that?

MAL: But isn't it a means of expression as well – and sometimes a
fuck or two's essential.
(MAN ON LEDGE *sighs.*)
Even if it's not . . . socially acceptable to you – and the likes
of you. But here you are – here's something to think about –
what would you rather have – a shit or a fuck?

MAN ON LEDGE: Oh Christ.

MAL: You'd rather have a blasphemy? . . . Look – take those
bastard buddy-buddy movies – Burt Reynolds and Clint
Eastwood and all boys together – Newman and Redford –
Butch and Sundance – what do they do? – they jump off a
stupid sheer face thousand-foot cliff edge – and what do they
shout? Do they shout 'Oh ffffuuuuucckkk!' No. Do they
perhaps acknowledge that they might be dimbo macho bank-
robbing bastards whose horses are shagged out – and whose
better days are behind them – do they take this final
opportunity for apology? – no – they shout
'Sssssshhhhiiiitttt!' (*Whispers. Exhausted.*) Shit is allowed.
Shit is acceptable. A fuck isn't. And I'm sorry if that makes
you unhappy. Or want to kill yourself. Kill yourself for a
fuck if I were you. I wouldn't kill myself for a shit. Not even
if I loved him.

MAN ON LEDGE: (*Soberly, at first*) I think you misjudge me, but it
hardly matters . . . and . . . I'll tell you this much . . . I loathe

29

... I loathe and despise what we have ... become ... how small we now all are ... how trivial and tiny we have been made to become ... I despair with every casual crudity of mouth and action I hear and ... witness, every scoundrel I see successful, every opportunity closed, every job lost, every resignation ... not tendered, every sign of the end of ... every decent principle.

MAL: At last you've said something I can understand.

MAN ON LEDGE: – Things that happen out there ... not even the wicked and terrible events – merely the everyday madness. Cuttings ripped from newspapers, things people say, been collecting them for years – (MAN ON LEDGE *opens his briefcase. Puts his hand in, then hesitates.*) – Like Sandy Gall at the end of part one on *News at Ten* one night said, 'And Daphne Du Maurier dies in Cornwall, that's in two minutes ...'
(MAL *laughs. The* MAN ON LEDGE *mournfully begins the* News at Ten *identity.*) ... But then, eventually, like the reaction you can build up to a drug or alcohol ... everything I'd ever kept couldn't keep me from what I could no longer face ... from the ways of the world (*Laughs*) – the state of the nation ... (*Begins to break up.*) ... And ... the knowledge of my own mor ... mortality ... and that ... those ... are too much to bear!

MAL: And that's a reason to die?

MAN ON LEDGE: But don't you see, it's killing me. All this waiting to die ... I've reached the point where I'm spending my days and nights – *my life* – waiting, taking my mind off the absolute inevitable, the approach of the ... final full stop at the end of the sentence, removing the curse so successfully at times that I ... actually turn those long days waiting into ... (*Perplexed laughter.*) ... fast and happy and wonderful times, short times ... thus, I don't know, hastening the process.

MAL: But do you think falling off this building is going to be ... *slow*?

MAN ON LEDGE: (*Agitated, hardly listening*) ... All my ... all my life, since ... since I found out that you die, all my life I've been building up and building up, knowing just knowing the certainty of my own mortality, yet – yet I can't believe that the day will ever come when I won't be alive! I know – I know everything's a mess out there – but it's a lot better than being dead – I know – I know – I know – yet – yet – yet – I know that that day will come – and I don't want it to come without warning – I don't want to be there if that happens – I can't take that – *I want the decision – and I can't stand waiting any longer!* (*He starts trying to find the courage to step off.*)

MAL: Oh fuck, he's going! WAIT! WAIT!

(*The* MAN ON LEDGE *laughs. As* MARTIN *enters Mal's flat. He is a small man. He is dressed loudly for golf. With golf bag. Looks bewildered at the carnage. Holds the door up. Puts his golf bag down. As we hear* UPRIGHT *and* UPSIDE DOWN *screaming and hurtling past the doorway to the flat.* MARTIN *turns and watches them. Goes to the doorway.* MARTIN *arrives in time to see the* BRUTES *giving chase with their sledgehammers.* MARTIN *looks bewildered and goes into the corridor. As the* MAN ON LEDGE *takes the briefcase off his head and teeters and tries. As* MAL *leans out to look up. As* UPRIGHT *and* UPSIDE DOWN *begin to back on to the flat roof. Being followed by the* TWO BRUTES.)

FIRST BRUTE: Up the stairs and say your prayers.

SECOND BRUTE: Get to the top and then down you drop.

UPRIGHT: They're *both* fuckin' mental.

FIRST BRUTE: You are going to die!

MAN ON LEDGE: *Yes!*

MAL: *No!*

(*As* MAL *begins to climb up towards the sixth floor. As* MARTIN *hears* MAL's *scream of 'No!' And goes to the window. Opens the window. As the* MAN ON LEDGE *puts one foot in mid-air. As if testing the air. Pulls it back at the last second but still building up for one very last effort. See* MARTIN *leaning out of the window. Sees* MAL.)

MARTIN: *Mal!*

MAL: *Martin – he's going to jump!*

MAN ON LEDGE: *I'm going to jump!*

(*All scream.* UPSIDE DOWN *and* UPRIGHT *have been backed up to the railings.*

UPSIDE DOWN *throws himself over the railings easily.*
UPRIGHT *gets there and hesitates. He turns to face the railings,*
turns back to face the BRUTES. *Turns back to the railings. But*
too late. UPRIGHT *is picked up by both* BRUTES *and lifted over*
and then on to the railings. He is left dangling by his coat collar.
UPSIDE DOWN *begins to climb down towards the sixth floor. His*
feet kick out towards Mal's head. MAL *screams.* UPSIDE DOWN
screams. MARTIN *screams.* UPRIGHT *is already screaming. The*
BRUTES *look over the railings. And scream.*)

BOTH BRUTES: IT WASN'T US!

(*While the* MAN ON LEDGE *tries again to go.*) Goodbye.

MAL: (*As she dangles*) OH FFFFFUUUUUCCCCCKKKKK!
(*Both* BRUTES *run away.*)

MARTIN: Mal!

MAL: Martin!

UPSIDE DOWN: Mam!

UPRIGHT: Mummy!

MAN ON LEDGE: Mortal! Mortal! *Yes!*

(*The lights go out and the curtain drops – a split second* after *the*
MAN ON LEDGE *has hurled himself into space.*)

ACT TWO

As was at the end of Act One.

  Except: UPSIDE DOWN *is clambering on to the sixth floor, where he then positions himself to take hold of* UPRIGHT *on his shoulders. He will lift him off the railings and allow* UPRIGHT *to climb down him and on to the sixth-floor ledge. And* MAL *is swinging back on to the fifth-floor ledge.*

  While: The MAN ON LEDGE *is standing in the hydraulic platform of the hoist as it rises into vision. He looks apparently alone, bewildered and frustrated by his failure. He looks down and attempts to get out and jump again. And a fireman's hand appears from inside the hydraulic platform and drags him back in.*

MOEY: (*Out of vision*) Fuckin' fuckin' fuckin' hell . . .
    (MOEY *staggers and climbs into sight in the hydraulic platform. He has one hand holding his helmeted head and the other still holding the* MAN ON LEDGE.)

MAN ON LEDGE: I did it. I did it. I jumped. I did it. I should be dead.

MOEY: Too fuckin' true.

MAN ON LEDGE: But it's not fair – a lot of really evil people who didn't want to die still died – and I'm still alive – it's not fair!
    (*Tries to get out. Dragged back by* MOEY.)

MOEY: Stay there.
    (*As* MAL *hauls herself back on to the fifth floor. And* UPRIGHT *is a gibbering wreck in* UPSIDE DOWN's *arms. And* MOEY *sees* MARTIN *inching along.*)
    Oh no, not Nick Faldo as well . . .

UPRIGHT: Help, help! I've got money, help me!

UPSIDE DOWN: We both have!

UPRIGHT: Help me!

MAN ON LEDGE: Let me go!

UPRIGHT: I'm sorry we kidnapped you.

MAN ON LEDGE: And I'm sorry I fell on your head, but –

UPRIGHT: Please, please help me.

MAN ON LEDGE: Just let me go.

(MOEY *looks from* UPRIGHT *to the* MAN ON LEDGE.)

UPRIGHT: I'll do anything.

MAN ON LEDGE: LET ME GO!

(MAN ON LEDGE *struggles to climb out of the platform.* MOEY *looks up, looks down, looks sideways. Moves his body to best hide his future intentions.*)

UPRIGHT: Fuck him – what about me?

(MOEY *takes out his fireman's axe, hits the* MAN ON LEDGE *with the blunt end.* MAN ON LEDGE *keels over slowly and lies on the bottom of the platform.*)

. . . I think I'm all right, actually.

MOEY: I take it everyone else wants to stay up here?

MARTIN: Mal – what is happening?

MOEY: Yeah, come on, Mal – a fuckin' resumé of recent events would not go amiss. Miss.

MARTIN: *Mal.*

MAL: I can't tell you, Martin. Not yet. Not here.

(MARTIN *edges nearer, holding out his hand.*)

MARTIN: Well, come back inside.

(MOEY *begins to descend with the* MAN ON LEDGE.)

MAL: That's something else I can't do . . . I'm sorry, Martin, I shouldn't have involved . . . but for the time being I'm staying here.

MOEY: Personally, I don't blame you. Being up here is becoming more fuckin' attractive by the minute. They're evil down there – evil – you're only off your fuckin' cakes. (*Looks down at the* MAN ON LEDGE *inside his hoist.*) Isn't it a funny world? – the only person up here who wants to die – I save his fuckin' life . . . anyone got any headache tablets? . . .

(MOEY *descends in the hoist.* MARTIN *reaches* MAL. *Hugs her. She barely responds.*)

MARTIN: What is it? What's the matter?

MAL: I can't tell you.

(MAL *shakes her head. While* UPRIGHT *just shakes.*)

UPRIGHT: I can't . . . stop . . . shakin' . . . Even me voice is . . . shakin'.

UPSIDE DOWN: Y'll get used to it.

UPRIGHT: Shakin'?

UPSIDE DOWN: No, bein' up here.

UPRIGHT: (*Still shaking*) You mean eventually – like in terms of
 . . . decades – like me fuckin' obituary'll read 'For the last
 fifty-six years of his life he lived on a ledge in Liverpool . . .'
 (*Points down without looking.*) And those bastards down
 there'll still be there – the only chance we've got, Billy, is if
 we outlive them.

UPSIDE DOWN: But y'will, y'll get used to it – just like we're goin'
 to get used to bein' rich.

UPRIGHT: But I haven't got a head for heights – I haven't even
 got a head for hats.

UPSIDE DOWN: We'll buy trilbys – any fucker can look good in a
 trilby. Y'wear a trilby – y'someone, lah – *someone*.

UPRIGHT: (*Gaining in confidence and forgetting where he is
 momentarily*) Yeah. Yeah. Someone. See, someone. As of
 now. Y'right. If I live long enough to walk the streets
 tomorrow, I'll be someone all right. An' then I won't be
 walkin' the streets. I'll be walkin' the fuckin' avenues an'
 lanes.

UPSIDE DOWN: Yis! And just remember, Jimmy, the secret is not
 to look down.

 (UPRIGHT *immediately looks down.*)

UPRIGHT: Yeah. Aaaaaaahhhhhhh.

 (UPRIGHT *nearly falls. Resorts to* UPSIDE DOWN's *arms for
 comfort and safety.*)

UPSIDE DOWN: Relax – just think about what's in your pockets.

MARTIN: Look, Mal –

MAL: (*Looking up*) Obviously you've got the money.

MARTIN, UPSIDE DOWN *and* UPRIGHT: What money?

MAL: You're welcome to it. Well, not you two in particular,
 but . . .

UPSIDE DOWN: We're welcome to it!

UPRIGHT: Oh fuck, I'm shakin' even more now.

UPSIDE DOWN: But it's ours. She said so.

UPRIGHT: But why doesn't she want it – what's wrong with it?

UPSIDE DOWN: Nothin'. Not now it's ours! I'm going to count it.

 (UPSIDE DOWN *attempts to pull the bags out of his pockets, while* UPRIGHT *still clings to him.*)

. . . Well, I'm gonna feel it anyway.

(*He feels the bags in one of his pockets.* UPRIGHT *gingerly feels the bag in* UPSIDE DOWN'*s other pockets.* UPSIDE DOWN *pushes his hand away.*)

UPSIDE DOWN: Feel your own money . . .

MARTIN: All right, you're not going to tell me, are you?

(MAL *shakes her head.*)

OK, well then, I'm going to tell you something – something I've been wanting to tell you for a long time –

MAL: Don't.

MARTIN: I've decided. And before you say anything – I know I don't decide very often, but this time I have – decided – and I want you and the – where are the kids?

MAL: At my mother's.

MARTIN: Are they safe?

MAL: Huh, a lot safer than if they were here.

MARTIN: I saw the door. Who would want to do a thing like that to a door?

MAL: You don't know me, Martin . You think you do, but you don't. Not the half. Look, I'm sorry, there was no one else I could, as they say, turn to. I just shouldn't have turned – brought you into all this . . . this . . . What did you tell Jean?

MARTIN: *Don't* ask me.

MAL: Come on, what did you tell her?

MARTIN: I, er . . . I, er, told her that they'd invented floodlit golf and I was going to give it a try.

MAL: I definitely shouldn't have asked you.

MARTIN: But I'm here now.

MAL: Go now.

MARTIN: But here's where I want to be – so listen to me – I've got something to tell you.

MAL: Martin.

MARTIN: Mal.

UPRIGHT: (*Nudging* UPSIDE DOWN, sotto voce) Fuckin' hell, it's like listenin' to a crossed line.

MARTIN: Mal, I've made my mind up. When we get off here – when I take you off here – I'm going to your mother's and

I'm going to take, I'll take . . .

MAL: Johnny.

MARTIN: Johnny. I'll say, I'll go home with him and I'll tell, I'll say to . . .

MAL: Jean.

MARTIN: I know! I know! Christ, I know my own wife's name. But I will, and I'll do more than that – I'll present him to – to – *her* – Jean Jean – well, I'll lock him in the car and I'll show him to her, in case she tries to kill him – I'll say 'Jean', I'll say, 'Jean, this is *my* son, Jean. Not yours, not ours – but mine' – I won't mention you just yet – but I'll tell her – 'MY SON! THIS IS MY SON!'

MAL: And what do you think she'll say to that?

MARTIN: . . . I don't think it's a good idea. I don't think I'll go home. I'll write. I'll write instead. Yeah. I know what to write, I've practised it countless times. I'll write – listen to this, Mal, see what you think – I'll write, 'Jean. *Dear* Jean . . . I'VE ALWAYS HATED YOU, JEAN!'

MAL: Stop this, stop it.

MARTIN: 'It's too late to stop, my mind is made up, I know where I want to be – I wanna be here with Mal.'

MAL: Martin, please –

MARTIN: 'I've always hated you, Jean! Even when we were courting! Oh yes!'

MAL: I think I'll jump.

MARTIN: 'So clever, Jean. So stuck-up clever, you bastard, Jean! I should have known then, all those years ago – I should have known on Decimalization Day! Yes, Decimalization Day!'

UPSIDE DOWN: *Wha'?*

UPRIGHT: It's, er, a Holy Day in the Common Market.

MARTIN: 'Seven times you corrected me that day! Seven times! Even Jesus only got denied three times, but you, you Jean, seven times you corrected me! "No, not a sixpence, Martin dear, Don't say two shillings, darling, and that's not a half a crown any more; what do you mean, Martin, where have all the threepenny bits gone? There's no such thing as nineteen and eleven any more, sweetheart." Just because you worked in a fuckin' bank, Jean. And there's worse. There's

Christmas Eve, 1969! I know I never had a proper education, Jean, what were four 'O' levels in those days? And I was glad – glad, do you understand glad . . .' Where was I?

UPRIGHT: Glad on Christmas Eve, 1969. Love to be there when she gets that fuckin' letter.

MAL: Martin –

MARTIN: 'The Chung Wah Chinese Restaurant, Lime Street, I met you off the train from Cheltenham, you had chicken chow mein with special fried rice, I had steak, chips and peas – I didn't know – nobody told me – you wouldn't have known neither unless you'd been to a fucking ladies' college – All I did, Jean, all I did was finish my meal and cross my knife and fork on the plate. That was all I did! And I'll never forget, how could you do it to me, you leant across and put my knife and fork side by side on my empty plate, and then you said – you said, "That's the civilized thing to do, Martin."'

UPRIGHT: . . . Fuckin' hell, is that all?

MARTIN: 'I wanted to kill you there and then but . . . but I married you instead. So I'm staying here, Jean, I want to be with . . . with . . . oh fuck! – With Mal and Johnny and her daughter, her daughter by someone else, and I don't want to live any more lies, Jean, and I don't care. I don't care if you think it's immoral because you would, you and your fuckin' Nat-West morality – because I wanna be free, I wanna be with Mal, I wanna have beliefs, I wanna be decent, I wanna care, you can't fuckin' well care in Southport! . . . With all best wishes, Martin' . . . What do you think, Mal? I mean, the grammar's probably all over the place, but –

(MAL *has ended up on her haunches, some distance away, with her hand over her face.*)

MAL: . . . Listen to me, Martin, please listen – Christ, why don't people listen to each other, Martin – I don't –

MARTIN: Don't what? I don't like don'ts, Jean Mal. Don't don't me.

MAL: You . . . you couldn't live with me, Martin.

MARTIN: Couldn't . . . couldn't I?

MAL: No.

MARTIN: But why not? There's room.

MAL: Actually, there's not, but –

MARTIN: We'll get a bigger place, I'll make more money, I'll drive a taxi in my spare time.

UPRIGHT: That'll get you fuck all in this city.

MARTIN: We'll manage.

MAL: Look, you're the father of my – my – oh Jesus!

UPRIGHT: Son. Name of Johnny . . . Is this catchin' or wha'?

MARTIN: Trust me, Mal, I've done the hard part, I'm free, I've crossed all my bridges and blown them up behind me, all we have to do now is live happily ever after.

MAL: Martin – *you don't know me.*

MARTIN: Well . . . tell me, make me understand.

MAL: I hardly know myself. Although I know a bit more since I . . . stepped out here. But . . . what do you think happens to me – what do you think I do when you're not here – there?

MARTIN: I . . . well I . . . I don't know.

MAL: I'm not blaming you, Martin, I'm not – it takes two to tangle – but come on, a girl cannot live by flying visits alone.

MARTIN: But all that's over now, Mal. I'm here. I'm here to stay. Here with you! (*Looks around. Looks down.*) But we won't be here for long because – (*Double-takes upon his look down.*) Is this . . . is this a regular event?

(MOEY *returns apparently alone in the fireman's hoist. Manoeuvres the platform close to* MAL. MOEY *looks at her, shrugs and turns away. Faces out.* SHAUN *peeps out from the platform and then stands up.*)

SHAUN: *What are you doing to me?*

MARTIN: Excuse me –

SHAUN: *Who the fuck are you?* And if you're a journalist, this woman is deranged, not one word is true and I'm here strictly on humanitarian grounds.

MARTIN: No, I'm a teacher, but –

SHAUN: Poor bastard. (*Turns directly to* MAL.) *What are you doing to me?*

MAL: Hopefully about the same as you're doing to this city, Shaun.

(SHAUN *laughs easily. No edge.*)

39

SHAUN: All right, anything you want, Mal. Anything. Anything I can do. Just give me back what is rightfully mine.

MAL: Rightfully? *Rightfully?*

UPRIGHT: Oh fuck, it's *his* money. It's important money.

SHAUN: There's no need for this – all we have to do is talk.

MARTIN: Excuse me.

MAL: Talk away.

SHAUN: How can I?

MARTIN: No really, excuse me –

SHAUN: Come on, kid. Good times. Think of the good times.

MARTIN: *What good times?*

SHAUN: Don't forget those good times.

MAL: Nah, you only get to seduce me the once, Shaun.

MARTIN: Er, hang on a minute –

SHAUN: All right. I tried charm, fuck you – get in there and give me back what you've got. *Now!*

MARTIN: Hey – hey – don't you talk to . . . er, to my friend like that. Who do you think you are? – and before you start, I sort of know who you are – I've seen you before – I'm not good at remembering things but it'll come to me. However, in the, er, meantime, this person here.

MOEY: Mal.

MARTIN: Mal is a close personal friend of mine, and . . . er, basically, don't talk to her like that. Understand?

SHAUN: (*To* MAL) Look, you –

MARTIN: Now that's –

(SHAUN *leans forward abruptly, grabs* MARTIN *by the testicles.*)

SHAUN: I'll cut you from arsehole to breakfast time if you don't shut up.

(SHAUN *pushes* MARTIN *back against the wall and returns to a kneeling position.*)

MARTIN: You're a politician! No, you're not a politician, you're that property developer! That's right. You've been in the papers recently – I remember now – you're being investigated. You're in trouble.

SHAUN: Trouble? You don't know what trouble is – fuckin' chalk pusher – fuckin' protected species – fuck off.

MARTIN: *I have to deal with sixteen-year-olds!*

(SHAUN *turns to* MOEY, *who, apart from when* SHAUN *grabbed* MARTIN, *has had his back turned throughout*.)

SHAUN: Hey you – get me on that ledge. *You.*

(MOEY *moves the platform nearer to the ledge*.)

MARTIN: Oh God, it's arsehole to breakfast time . . .

(MARTIN *edges along the ledge towards Mal's window. Goes to step inside. Sees the two* BRUTES *suddenly framed before him in the flat. The* FIRST BRUTE *waves wanly at* MARTIN. *As* MARTIN *returns along the ledge.* SHAUN *gets on the ledge*.)

SHAUN: So here I am – I'm asking nicely. So give me what you've got and we'll call it quits.

MAL: . . . Why did you give it to me?

SHAUN: (*Quietly*) You shouldn't have read the contents.

MAL: *Why did you give it to me?*

SHAUN: (*Very quietly*) Because I thought I could trust you, because I was . . . ducking for cover, because the Fraud Squad and the Inland Revenue started seizing everything they could find, but most of all, because . . . I thought I could trust you.

MAL: You gave me filth.

SHAUN: It's business.

MAL: Corruption, degradation, bribery, violence?

SHAUN: (*Nods*) Business.

MAL: Well, I didn't want to know, Shaun, like too fucking many of us, I just didn't want to know. But now that I do –

SHAUN: Forget you know.

MAL: I can't. How can I forget?

SHAUN: Look, give me the papers. You keep the money. Take it as a bonus.

(MAL *stares at him*.)

A farewell present. Mal, I don't care about the money.

(UPRIGHT *and* UPSIDE DOWN *look at each other. Joyously*.)

UPRIGHT: *He doesn't care about the money!*

(UPRIGHT *and* UPSIDE DOWN *begin to edge back*.)

MAL: Why should you care – there'll be plenty more where that came from, no doubt, but what I can't forget is what you've done –

SHAUN: Oh fuck that, save that for the front of house and the

41

party political broadcasts. We're all out here on our own.

MAL: That's not true.

MOEY: (*Still facing out*) You said two minutes.

SHAUN: (*Without looking*) I'll give you overtime.

MAL: He paid you to bring him up here? (*Silence.*) He did, didn't he?

MOEY: (*Without turning*) Of course he paid me. Every man has his price. And I was going cheap.

(*As* SHAUN *proceeds, see* MOEY *dropping ten-pound notes from the platform. Expressionless.*)

SHAUN: Don't come the sweet innocent now, Mal. You knew.

UPRIGHT: (*Pointing*) Money.

UPSIDE DOWN: Oh don't be so greedy.

UPRIGHT: You're supposed to be greedy.

SHAUN: You knew all right. After all, you were, considering where you come from, sophisticated. You knew who I was when I picked you up – you knew what I did when I bedded you –

MARTIN: Er, excuse me.

SHAUN: You weren't innocent then. You didn't complain then.

MAL: Of course I didn't –

SHAUN: Well then –

MAL: Because you were my tart, Shaun.

SHAUN *and* MARTIN: WHAT?

MAL: *Really* sophisticated women, so I've been told, that's what they call someone like you, Shaun. Their tart. Horrible, isn't it?

MARTIN: Mal, we've got a lot of very serious talking to do.

SHAUN: I'm nobody's tart!

MOEY: And neither am I. Your time's up.

SHAUN: (*Without looking*) I'll double what I gave you.

MOEY: No thanks. I've heard enough.

(SHAUN *finally turns to him.*)

SHAUN: What do you want? *What do you want?*

MOEY: Nothing you can give me, bollocks. I'm merely not as cheap as I thought I was.

SHAUN: You can't do that to me. Not without there being consequences.

(MOEY *moves the platform further away.*)

MOEY: . . . You were saying?

> (SHAUN *points at* MOEY. *Then points at* MAL. *Points back at* MOEY. *Words fail him. Almost. He nods and indicates for the hoist to return.*)

SHAUN: (*Lightly, as he climbs into the hoist*) You know, if I got to know you any better, I'd find your weakness – and play upon it. You have got a weakness haven't you?

MOEY: (*Flatly*) I'm an Everton supporter.

SHAUN: (*To* MAL) I'll . . . I'll be back.

UPRIGHT: I wish a tart'd say that to me one day.

SHAUN: I'll win, Mal. No rules when I play.

MOEY: Y'ever played for Wimbledon? Arsenal? (*Turns away. He slowly begins to take the platform down.*) A circus came to this estate last year. Only lasted twenty-four hours. Circus owner woken up in the middle of the night by the sound of howling. Hordes of kids tryin' to open the lions' cage. It's true. Fuckin' lions lyin' there terrified, huddled up in the far corner, goin' – 'No, not them, keep those fuckin' savages away – fuck this "King of the Jungle" lark around here – we wanna go back to Hampshire . . .'

> (MOEY *disappears from sight.* SHAUN *has already knelt down in the hoist.* MARTIN *gets closer to* MAL.)

MARTIN: . . . Now will you talk to me?

MAL: In intimate detail? No, no. You should go. I'm sorry.

MARTIN: Go – after all that? Is it true? Is it? Him? You –

MAL: It's a . . . fact.

MARTIN: Bugger me – when did you find the time?

MAL: When you weren't there, Martin. When you weren't here. When you were *never* here. *Years* can go by that way – years *have* gone by that way – the countless Saturdays you were forced screaming to Safeways and the shopping arcades of Southport – instead of being here with me – the Sundays Jean wanted you to go to the Lake District at the last minute instead of being here with me – I mean, fucking hell, Martin, you must have squatting rights in Keswick, Kendal and Windermere – the fortnights you spent in France with your family – instead of being here with me – on and on and on.

43

But most of all, when you got up and washed your body and left me. To go home. And I would get out of that bed and get dressed. And I would leave my children at my mother's . . . and I would go to town. *And I mean go to town* . . . in anger and some kind of desire . . . hatred even . . . and it was that hatred of you – and me – that brought me back to his hotel bedroom one night . . . after you had washed your body of the smell of me . . . and then left me . . . but isn't what I've got here – in here – more important than . . . that?

MARTIN: No – fuck that – this is – this is . . . me and you . . . us.

MAL: But this is me and you as well. This is me and you and half a million people out there.

MARTIN: But I don't care! I don't, Mal. I'm a woodwork teacher. And I've got a terrible memory and a lousy marriage and things like that don't interest me anyway. You said yourself that was one of the things you liked about me – you could escape with me – WHY DIDN'T YOU TELL ME?
(*Silence.* MAL *looks away.*)
About him? You and him? How long has this been going on?
(UPRIGHT *begins to sing 'How long has this been going on'.*
UPSIDE DOWN *joins in with a snatch of the verse and dance movements.*)

UPRIGHT: It's fuckin' sound up here, isn't it? I think I'll come here tomorrow night. I think I'll live here.

UPSIDE DOWN: You might have to.

MARTIN: (*Like a little boy, lost*) Why didn't you tell me?

MAL: Why didn't you tell Jean – until now – when you've told the whole world? I'll tell you why, Martin – for the same reason I never told you – for the fear that whoever you tell will be a bucket of tears. And you don't quite care enough about . . . whoever you tell to have the bucket of tears thrown back all over you . . . It was selfish of me. And it was selfish of me to bring you here tonight. More than that – it was awful – maybe that's even why I did it . . . Just go home.

MARTIN: Home? But home is where the heartache is. I can't go home.

MAL: Yes you can.

MARTIN: Even if . . . even if I wanted to, there's a brute of a bloke

44

in there who won't let me go home.

MAL: He'll let you go. It's me he really wants.

UPRIGHT *and* UPSIDE DOWN: And me.

MAL: Go home and talk to Jean.

(MARTIN *looks at* MAL *in disbelief*.)

How long is it since you talked to Jean?

UPRIGHT: Decimalization Day . . .

(MARTIN *takes a step away from* MAL. *Then stops and returns*.)

MARTIN: What about Johnny?

MAL: He'll be here. He's ours.

MARTIN: I'll . . . I'll be back.

MAL: Course you will.

(*She kisses him on the cheek*.)

MARTIN: I will. (*Moves away. Stops*.) I don't wanna go. *I'm not going!* I'm a good . . . I mean, I'm good, I'm one of life's good guys. Good guys don't walk away like this. They stay. They say – 'I'm staying.' And they stay.

MAL: Gary Cooper's dead, Martin. So's Tommy Cooper.

MARTIN: . . . I'll come back . . . (*Gets to the window*.) And then I'll stay. I promise. I'll . . . come back.

MAL: Yeah – the men in my life always say that – either as a threat or a promise.

(MARTIN *edges off the ledge into* MAL's *flat. As he does so, we hear one of the Brutes' phones ringing.* FIRST BRUTE *takes his phone out and holds it to his ear*.)

FIRST BRUTE: I'm getting the hang of this . . . (*Answers*.) . . . Yeah, yeah, as we speak. (*Looks to* MARTIN.) Will do.

(*The* FIRST BRUTE *snatches* MARTIN, *tickles him under the arms, lifts him into* MAL's *flat, turns him against the window and body-searches him*.)

MARTIN: Gerroff!

FIRST BRUTE: A man must have his pleasures . . . Mmmmm, very trim, and well hung –

(*The* FIRST BRUTE *goes to close the window. Looks along the ledge to* MAL. *Grins*.)

Extremely well hung.

(*He closes the window, gets hold of* MARTIN *by the scruff of his neck. Marches him to the doorway and out*.)

45

Tell me, have you ever been locked in a car with a dented head?

UPRIGHT: . . . What're we gonna do now?

UPSIDE DOWN: Spend our money.

UPRIGHT: I didn't know Dixons had a branch up here. (*Looks around the ledge.*)

UPSIDE DOWN: You know – in our heads. Imagine like. What we're gonna spend our money on. I've spent loads already.

UPRIGHT: I'd rather get off here and spend it properly. (*Looks gingerly to his side.*) There has to be another window open somewhere.

UPSIDE DOWN: We could go window-shopping! (*Laughs. Alone.*) Come ahead, let's look.

UPRIGHT: . . . I don't think I can move. Not without a written guarantee . . . or a hand to hold.

(UPSIDE DOWN *offers his hand.* UPRIGHT *looks at it. Reluctantly takes hold of it.*)

If you ever tell anyone that I held your hand . . .

(*They begin to move off, stage right.*)

What've you spent your money on so far?

UPSIDE DOWN: Your engagement ring, darling.

(UPRIGHT *grabs his hand away, teeters.* UPSIDE DOWN *grabs him.*)

UPRIGHT: *I'm serious.* Ever since our Joey was found huddled in me mother's wardrobe, I've been worried it might run in the family.

UPSIDE DOWN: He'll grow out of it – I did.

(UPRIGHT *looks sharply at him.*)

Nah, lads, when they're little, often like dressin' up like that.

UPRIGHT: Our Joey's thirty-four – with a fuller figure and size twelve stilettos. (*Shakes his head.*) So, if this gets out, I'm warnin' you.

UPSIDE DOWN: It won't get out. No one'll see us here. They'll all be fire-bombin' the Conservative Club an' ram-raidin' Woolworths.

UPRIGHT: Ye –

(UPRIGHT *looks down. Goes dizzy with fear and vertigo. Still holding hands with* UPSIDE DOWN.)

Hah . . . hah . . . tell me what you're really going to buy – go
on – take my mind off – off – off all this *height*.

UPSIDE DOWN: I'm gettin' a flyin' jacket, deffo.

(UPRIGHT *nearly passes out*. UPSIDE DOWN *pulls him back
against the wall*.)

I know what I really want, lah! I want a suit with a foreign
name. Ohhhh!

UPRIGHT: A foreign name?

UPSIDE DOWN: Yeah!

UPRIGHT: Like . . . Brussels?

UPSIDE DOWN: Nah. Nah! Like y'can't pronounce. Like Italian.
Like . . . what a footballer wears for Inter Milan.

UPRIGHT: Blue and green – with an advertisement for Spaghetti
Hoops across your chest?

UPSIDE DOWN: Nah. Like what he wears when he's in a disco . . .
Like later when he's in bed with a beautiful blonde and the
suit's lying there all crumpled on the floor. *And it still looks
smart.*

(UPSIDE DOWN *is about to take* UPRIGHT *around the corner
and off*.)

UPRIGHT: I want . . . I want . . . I want . . .

(*The two* BRUTES *promptly appear around the other corner of
the sixth-floor ledge*.)

FIRST BRUTE: A priest, that's what you want.

(UPRIGHT *and* UPSIDE DOWN *panic and flee*. FIRST *and*
SECOND BRUTE *begin to pursue them. Hear the sound of a
portable phone*. FIRST BRUTE *takes it out of his pocket*.)

Hello . . . hello?

(FIRST BRUTE *butts the phone. Still hear the sound of portable
phone ringing*. SECOND BRUTE *holds his hand out*.)

SECOND BRUTE: Here, let me have a go.

(FIRST BRUTE *reluctantly hands him the phone*.)

Hello?

(*Truth slowly dawns. It is the Second Brute's phone that is
ringing. He hands the* FIRST BRUTE *his phone back. Takes his
phone out. Presses button and listens*.)

. . . Is right . . . Is right! . . . Is correct. (*Puts phone away,
stares*.)

FIRST BRUTE: . . . And?

SECOND BRUTE: Me tea's ready.

FIRST BRUTE: (*In anger, as they go off, following* UPRIGHT *and* UPSIDE DOWN) Course y'tea's ready – my tea's always ready – that's what y'get married for – but you're a professional now – the days of wine and roses are over – romance is about to leave your life – now y'a professional – and there's one golden rule for a professional – a professional sometimes has to sacrifice his tea! Come 'head.

(*And they go off around the building. As the* MAN ON LEDGE *appears around the other corner of the sixth-floor ledge. He is shuffling, bewildered, hesitant, with a bandage around his head and his briefcase in his hand. He feels the bandage and winces. Looks around at his surroundings as he shuffles.*)

MAN ON LEDGE: . . . So . . . so I came up here . . . there was a lot of swearing . . . and . . . someone hit me. Someone hit me very hard.

MAL: Oh shit. Oh fuck, I said shit!

MAN ON LEDGE: . . . I went down there, that's right . . . but how did I get down there? . . . Someone else bandaged my head. And I ran away . . . *and I still want to go to the toilet* . . . But . . . but what I really want to know is . . . *who am I?* What was I . . . doing up here in the first place?

(MAL *looks up, as the* MAN ON LEDGE *opens his briefcase and looks at a cutting. Reads it and as he continues, we should be aware that, to his puzzlement, he is reciting extracts from his collection of cuttings.*)

. . . I don't . . . what . . . ? The *Dallas Daily News* – 'A Dallas man filming a road traffic safety movie on the dangers of low-level bridges was killed on Wednesday when the truck he was standing on passed under a bridge . . .'

(*The* MAN ON LEDGE *looks bewildered. Ducks and drops his briefcase. It narrowly misses* MAL *on the ledge beneath.*)

MAL: Oh my God!

MAN ON LEDGE: The *Stafford Mercury* – 'Twice as many people as expected turned out to a public lecture on schizophrenia . . .' Does . . . does that mean . . . ? Am I two people – one of whom was killed by a low-level bridge . . . ?

48

MAL: Listen to me. Please. Listen to me.

MAN ON LEDGE: (*Shakes his head and walks a pace or two*) And the voices, those voices. The *Brisbane Times* – 'One Million People in Australia Can't Read. Are You One of Them?' . . . But I can read . . . I think. (*Looks at his watch.*) Omega. Yes . . . what do . . . these mean . . . *to me*? Is it because – the *Yorkshire Post* – 'Leeds Magistrates were told yesterday that a man found with his trousers down and a woman astride him was arrested for impersonating a police officer.' Good God, what kind of a life have I – the *Daily Mail* – 'A man who stole a British Rail egg sandwich was ordered to see a psychiatrist because a magistrate doubted his sanity . . .' (*The* MAN ON LEDGE *turns the corner, still bewildered.*) . . . Sanity? Sanity? Psy . . . chiatrist . . . egg sandwich . . . ? (*As* MOEY *returns in his fireman's hoist . . . 'talking' as the platform rises.* MOEY *reaches for the ledge. Climbs on to the ledge. He takes off his helmet, tunic and gloves. Throws them into the hoist. He signals for the hoist to be taken away. It glides downwards.*)

MOEY: . . . I am *not* going down there again, fuck that! They attacked *me! Me!* . . . And what was I doing? What was my role in life on fourteen and a half thousand pounds a year plus overtime, heat-resistant clothing, singed eyebrows and third-degree burns – *I* was out there riskin' life an' fuckin' limb for the fuckin' idiots. And I live in Runcorn! Fuck that! . . . I don't believe them – have they all gone fuckin' mad – they're tryin' to fuckin' kill me for puttin' the fires out. Where they live. WHERE THEY LIVE!

MAL: . . . If you call it living.

(MOEY *sits down on the ledge angrily. Points at* MAL.)

MOEY: Oh, a fuckin' social worker. Don't start. Just don't start. I've come up here for sanctuary. I do not want to hear *anything* that resembles sociology. And I shall smack the next person I hear mention the word 'community'. (*He stands up, even angrier.*) I have tried to be a part of a community, even if the fuckin' community doesn't exist any more. And what's more, personally, I blame that John Cleese for all this. I fuckin' do. That fuckin' book he brought out – *How To Be*

Assertive or somethin'. It's all right for him – he's eight foot fuckin' six and the funniest man alive – he gets assertive? – everyone goes 'Hah hah hah, good old John, what a larf, anything you want, John.' Me or you get assertive – it's 'Who the fuck d'you think you're talking to!' (*He mimes giving and receiving a head butt as he speaks:*) Fuck off! And stitches in Casualty.

MAL: . . . Do you really believe that those poor sods down there have actually read John Cleese's book on assertiveness?

MOEY: Poor sods? They're not poor sods – they're evil stupid bastards!

(*As* UPRIGHT *and* UPSIDE DOWN *appear again around a corner on the sixth-floor ledge, looking carefully behind and in front of themselves.*)

UPRIGHT: Is he talkin' about us again?

MOEY: Oh fuckin' hell, its Prince William and Prince Harry!

MAL: No, you're wrong – whateveryournameis. What is your name? I hate proving I'm right to someone without a name.

MOEY: Moey.

UPRIGHT: It's short for Moët Chandon – his dad was pissed at the christening. Could have been worse – could have been called Tetley Walker.

MOEY: (*Looking up*) Maurice, and it wasn't my idea – but listen – *you're* wrong – I know about these things – I organized our local Neighbourhood Watch last year, didn't I? There'd been a spate – couldn't leave your house without chainin' down y'telly, y'curtains, an' y'carpet – held the first meeting in our front room – tea and biscuits, rotas and self-defence – it was great – fellers walkin' around holdin' their beer guts in and a baseball bat in their hand – three days later –

UPRIGHT: He got burgled.

MOEY: Yeah all right – go ahead – prove my point – but they found the feller though – oh aye – lived right across the road – been the meetin', hadn't he? Casin' the joint over his chocolate biscuits. 'Mmmmmmmmmm, that's a nice three-piece suite.' Still, I thought, that's the end of him . . . but no sense of shame, some people – one year, he got, six months suspended – the bastard came back to the street – just before

Christmas – bold as brass –
(UPRIGHT *and* UPSIDE DOWN *are about to turn the corner of the building.*)

UPRIGHT: All the kids in the street terrified to put their
Christmas stockings up . . .

(MOEY *sits down again as he talks.*)

MOEY: *And.* And he says 'Hello' to me every time I pass him.
Huh. Phoned me up last week, wantin' to know a good
smoke-alarm system. I told him 'Cancer' . . . I didn't
actually, he's a lot bigger than me – but that's another thing –
the phones – Christ, even the phones are out to get you, these
days. Remember when there used to be a nice gentle hum
when you picked up your phone to dial – 'Hi hello, I'm your
phone, I'll be gentle with you.' Now – *now* – there's this
strident aggressive high-pitched whine – 'WHAT DO YOU
WANT, YOU FUCKER?' (MOEY *has ended up standing
again. Sits down, puts his head in his hands.*) . . . All right,
OK, so it's not John Cleese's fault – but who's fault is it?

MAL: (*Quietly*) It's our fault – it's everybody's fault.

MOEY: I knew it – I fucking knew you'd say that. Don't. Just
don't.

MAL: We're all to blame.

MOEY: . . . And is that why you're up here? Because you're to
blame?

MAL: . . . I'm out here because I stopped turning the other cheek
. . . because I've got nowhere else to go. I'm safe out here.

MOEY: Well, if he's so dangerous to know, why did you get
involved with him in the first place?

MAL: Why did you take his money?

MOEY: I didn't let him fuck me.

MAL: (*Laughing*) That's where you're wrong – someone like him –
his position and power – his money and all its uses . . . power
is an aphrodisiac, Moey.

MOEY: Oh yeah?

MAL: Sure. You get to fuck everybody.

(MOEY *laughs in acknowledgement. As the* MAN ON LEDGE
returns on the sixth-floor ledge.)

MAN ON LEDGE: . . . The *New York Times* – 'The former Head

51

Chaplain of the Brooks Army Medical Center has pleaded guilty to charges of adultery, sodomy and wrongful use of a government telephone.' *What?*

MOEY: Oh, hey! How did he get back up here. Fuck me, you really don't have to die to come back and haunt people . . . (MOEY *tries to look up towards the sixth floor.*)

MAN ON LEDGE: *What does all this mean to me?*

MAL: (*Quietly*) I know.

MAN ON LEDGE: They're coming out like hiccups, and I can't – the problems page, *She Magazine* – 'I'm sorry to return to the problem of premature ejaculation, but my postbag is absolutely full of it' . . . sodomy . . . adultery . . . what kind of person am I?

MAL: (*Loudly*) I can tell you!

MOEY: Is this wise?

MAN ON LEDGE: (*Looking down*) Who are – Lost and Found column, the *Solihull News* – 'Lost – brown and black dog, has piebald left eye and limps, got half of right ear missing, and no tail. Answers to the name of "Lucky" . . .' (*Holds his mouth.*) . . . Who are you?

MAL: F'ing this and F'ing that and Daphne Du Maurier. Remember?

MAN ON LEDGE: Am I in a . . . home? Outside a . . . place for – ?

MAL: No, no, you – you – I know why you collect them – because the world is mad – you've been telling yourself for years – that's the proof – the world is mad – and you can join in and nobody will notice. Don't you see – they've kept you alive.

MAN ON LEDGE: Kept me – Jeffrey Archer – the *Guardian* – 'Yes, we've met two Kurds, we call them Lemon Kurd and Bean Kurd . . . ' Who is Jeffrey Archer?

MOEY: Fuckin' hell, I've just heard the perfect definition of 'ignorance is bliss'.

MAN ON LEDGE: . . . I don't . . . I don't understand.

MAL: Keep talking. Keep telling yourself. That's all you need to keep living. It's all crazy fucking tunes.

MAN ON LEDGE: . . . Swearing. I know I don't like that.

MAL: That's right.

MAN ON LEDGE: I don't know why. How do I know they're

swear words – oh, oh, I do want to go to the toilet . . . (*Takes a pace or two.*) . . . Are you really trying to help me?

MAL: YES!

MAN ON LEDGE: . . . Keep talking?

MAL: Yes.

MAN ON LEDGE: I can talk – why can't I remember – why can't I – J. Edgar Hoover, FBI Files – 'I regret to say that we of the FBI are powerless to act in cases of oral–genital intimacy unless it has in some way obstructed interstate commerce . . .' Lenny Bruce – 'All my humour is based on destruction and despair. If the whole world were tranquil, without disease and violence, I'd be standing in the breadline, right behind J. Edgar Hoover . . . '

(*The* MAN ON LEDGE *shakes his head as he turns the corner. As* MOEY *looks down, whistles and motions again.*)

MOEY: If I had kids growing up now . . . I wouldn't have kids. I know one thing, it wasn't like this when . . .

(MOEY *stops and looks wryly at* MAL. *Shrugs.*)

Well, it wasn't . . . (*Looks down.*) Come on, will y'? . . . How old are yours?

MAL: Five and three and a half. Moondance and Kylie.

(MOEY *double-takes.*)

Catherine and Johnny.

MOEY: Not easy.

(MAL *looks sourly at him.*)

No. You know, being on your own.

MAL: Was it ever easy? And please don't mention that 'single mothers' weren't that common when you were a kid.

MOEY: All right. Most of us had dads when I was a kid . . .

MAL: Well . . . I wish my kids had . . . two parents – come to think of it, collectively they've got three – but I know what you mean – about back then – when all our parents had . . . was us, the future, *our* future, the things that we were going to do – because our generation had a horizon offered to us, Moey. No other time – no other civilization in the history of the world ever appeared to hold out *real* prospects for the people –

MOEY: The common herd?

MAL: *The majority!*
> (MOEY *looks flatly away.*)
> Moey, we were born and brought up in a time when the
> horizon seemed to come closer!

MOEY: Being a fuckin' mirage, it would, wouldn't it?

MAL: No – no, you're wrong – barriers were being broken down –
> or seemed to be – and lack of class and accent or money – age
> even – *did not appear to matter.*

MOEY: I'd almost forgotten.

MAL: But promises were being made to the cannon fodder for the
> very first time that, being unused to attention, we believed,
> and we made promises to ourselves that –

MOEY: One day every home would have a colour television and a
> barbecue stand, while every fuckin' bar in Benidorm would
> sell San Miguel, Pina Colada and chicken in the basket.
> That's what we were being educated for.

MAL: . . . While we thought we were being educated for life.

MOEY: (*Gently*) We were, you soft sod. All our yesterdays, hey? I
> was happy then. I was happy there – I was happy here – I was
> happy every fuckin' where . . . I hate the past. *I hate the past*
> – cos I have to live in the *present*, never mind the future,
> while in the past I was happy – and that's not a dream world
> – it's a memory – my memory of when it was simple and safe
> and boring and *we thought we stood a chance* – huh, chance'd
> be a fine thing now. Christ, it's freezin' up here.
> (*As* UPRIGHT *and* UPSIDE DOWN *reappear around the corner.
> On their ledge. Happy, but still holding hands.*)

UPRIGHT: I want . . . I want . . . I know what I want! *I wanna go
> on a train!* I wanna go first class! Somewhere –
> anyfuckin'where – go past the fuckin' buffet car for once in
> my life. Past that snidy little barrier the bastards've put up
> . . . an' make a phone call from first class . . . 'Yeah, yeah,
> it's me, Mam, we've broken down just outside Stafford . . . '
> Brilliant. Fuckin' brilliant . . . It's really strange havin'
> somethin' to live for, isn't it?
> (*The boys are approaching the opposite corner. There is a huge
> explosion. It comes from where they all face out. All four jump in
> shock.* UPRIGHT *nearly loses his footing. They all stare out.*

MOEY *begins to look around*.)

UPSIDE DOWN: Jesus Christ, that's the Dole that's gone up!

UPRIGHT: It's a fuckin' Government plot! It fuckin' is. It's a reverse of the real Guy Fawkes bombin' fuckin' Parliament – only this time it's the Government bombin' the fuckin' people . . .

(UPSIDE DOWN *guides him around a corner*.)

You fuckin' watch, it'll be the launderettes next – and then the Leisure Centre . . .

(UPRIGHT *and* UPSIDE DOWN *go around a corner and off.* SHAUN *stands by Mal's window in her flat, watching and so far unseen. Opens the window. While* MOEY *climbs up to the sixth floor as he speaks, anxious to get a better view of the bedlam and mayhem.*)

MOEY: . . . Fuck me sideways . . . the place is one fire. They've gone one step on – the stupid fuckin' bastards are burnin' down where they live – *where they live*!

SHAUN: No they're not – they're burning down property – a considerable part of which belongs to me. ME!

(MAL *retreats from* SHAUN, *towards the drainpipe.* MOEY *points out in disbelief.*)

Mal, I'm not asking – I'm telling – give me those papers.

MAL: No.

(SHAUN *laughs in disbelief. Half steps on to the ledge.*)

SHAUN: Come on, we're better than all of this – why should you care?

MAL: *Because of these!* (MAL *takes some papers from out of the Tesco bag. Holds them out.*) And . . . and this . . . place. Here – here where cowboys can become kings. (*Looks to* SHAUN.) No, Shaun. No.

SHAUN: We'll see about that.

MOEY: That's the dingle that's on fire. I was born in the dingle.

(MAL *begins to climb towards the sixth ledge.* SHAUN *closes the window and hurries out of the flat.*)

That's the Dingle that's on fire. I was born in the Dingle.

MAL: Wanna know how easy it is to cheat *and* prosper – wanna get the planning permission before you buy the land – wanna turn a playing field into another fucking shopping precinct –

55

'Wanna woman in your room, sir – wanna holiday in Malta –
wanna flat in Malta – wanna buy fuckin' Malta?' (*Looks up
from the top of the drainpipe to* MOEY.) Wanna know how
much it is to rape a city? Murder a country –

MOEY: (*Helping her on to the sixth-floor ledge*) Yeah, yeah, I know
already – I fuckin' know.

MAL: Well of course you do – that's your style all right – know all
– *do* fuck all – like a eunuch makin' believe he's got a
hard-on –

MOEY: What? What?

MAL: Even worse than ignorance, Moey – cos when you know
everything – when that glorious day comes when you know
everything – there won't be anything left worth knowing
about!

MOEY: Oh, I've got to get off here.

As SHAUN *kicks and bursts open a boarded-up window on the
sixth floor near to both* MAL *and* MOEY. *He leers out at them,
without ever climbing on to the ledge.*)

SHAUN: (*To* MAL) Listen you – nobody gives you nothin' in this
world – you've got to take it – what is wrong with bein' a wolf
in wolf's clothing – hey? Cos I know where I come from,
Mal, and I'm never fuckin' well going back there! (*He looks
at her, exhausted by his actions and his passion. Whispers.*) . . .
Don't you see, I was crazy for you. (*He half turns away, as if
denying that he had spoken.*)

MAL: *What? What?*

SHAUN: (*Immediately back on the attack*) But you're up here where
you belong – in the fuckin' clouds. With all the other misfits
and missionaries and moaners and 'might-be merchants'.
Open your eyes, stupid. Look! Your friends, the deprived
and the depraved are fuckin' up again. AGAIN!

(SHAUN *points out. See a backdrop of increasing flames and
destruction. Also hear the ever-increasing sound of fire engines,
police sirens, ambulances. A distant helicopter sound is heard.*)

MAL: No – you did all of this.

MOEY: Even the trees are on fire.

MAL: You and everyone else who thinks like you – you did this.

SHAUN: Yeah, yeah, sure we did, winner takes all, but listen, soft

56

arse, for there to be winners there have to be losers – you lose again – so do me a favour – save the sanctity for the *New Statesman*. (*Looks to* MAL.) Twat, I loved you.
(*Hear a scream from the area of the roof. See the two* BRUTES *burst into sight. They bring* MARTIN *between them, his hands held behind his back.*)

MARTIN: Mal!
(*He is hit on the back by one of the* BRUTES. *He cries out. As he is brought to the railings,* MAL *tries to lean out to look.*)

MARTIN: Mal – what is happening?

SHAUN: I can probably help you here, Mal. My, er, associates are investigating the theory of downward projection with your – unfortunate friend.

MAL: Leave him alone – he knows nothing – he's done nothing.

SHAUN: I realize that – but he knows you – and I hope he knows how to fly, because in ten seconds he's going somewhere over the rainbow.

MARTIN: NO – NO!
(*One of the* BRUTES *hits* MARTIN *effortlessly on the back again.*)
Ahhhhhhhh! MAL!

MAL: It's OK, Martin –

MARTIN: I'M SCARED, MAL!

MAL: They won't hurt you.

MARTIN: THEY'RE ALREADY HURTING ME!

SHAUN: It's up to you, kid. He's ready for take-off.

MAL: Not even you would do this – there's too many witnesses.

SHAUN: Witnesses to what – we were trying to save his life, that's all – I heard him from down below – everyone heard him – a deranged man who was raving about how much he hated his wife and mourning the demise of pounds, shillings and pence.

MAL: *He's a witness.* (*Points to* MOEY.)

MOEY: Oh no – leave me out of this – I can't fly, I know I can't fly.

SHAUN: On your own again, good citizen Mal. Now give me those papers.

MOEY: (*To* MAL) I've got to get off here. (*Shouts down.*) Get me off here! (*To* MAL.) *Give him the fucking things!* (*Shouts down.*) Get me off here!
(*MAL stands as if to throw the contents of the bag away.*)

SHAUN: Throw that over, Mal, and your friend can read all about it on the way down. (*Looks up.*) Let's have lift-off, boys.

FIRST BRUTE: Right boss.

(*The* BRUTES *begin to swing* MARTIN *up and over the railings. Jauntily.*)

SHAUN: Ten.

MOEY: *Come on, who elected you, Joan of Arc?*

SHAUN: Nine.

MARTIN: MAL!

MAL: (*As she sees him being swung over the railings*) No!

MOEY: It isn't important.

MARTIN: NO! NO!

SHAUN: Eight.

MARTIN: PLEASE!

MOEY: Come on, I'm needed down there!

SHAUN: Seven.

MARTIN: HELP ME! HELP ME!

MAL: You bastard!

SHAUN: Nah nah – not me – no bastard me, still legitimate – that's me – *six*.

MAL: You won't –

SHAUN: Tart, hey?

MAL: You won't –

SHAUN: I'll give you tart. Five – four.

MARTIN: MAL! MAL!

MAL: You wouldn't –

MOEY: Give it to him, f'fuck's sake.

MAL: I . . . I . . .

MARTIN: PLEASE, PLEASE!

SHAUN: Three. If I say two and one really fast, he's dead, Mal.

MAL: But . . . but –

SHAUN: Two, Mal.

MAL: OK, OK.

MARTIN: JEAN!

MAL: . . . Enough.

(*She gives* SHAUN *the bag.*)

SHAUN: Very good. All right, boys, no more swings. Take-off aborted.

(*The* BRUTES *drop* MARTIN *with a dismissive, casual, sickening thump.*)

MAL: So is that it, Shaun? Is that what you're telling me – that we can tell anyone – tell the papers – tell the people – and see where it gets us?

SHAUN: Oh yes! Now that I've got this! (*Brandishes the documents from the bag.*)

MAL: That all that matters now is tits and innuendo – who's had a nose job – who's had a blow job – who gives a fuck about who's got no job – is that the secret – is it?

SHAUN: The lesson hath been learnt. (*He exits.*)
(*As the unmanned hoist appears see* SHAUN *leave the kicked-in window.*)

MOEY: Come on, come on –
(*As the helicopter lights rake* MAL *and* MOEY.)

MAL: I want to – (*Points up.*) Martin.

MOEY: See him downstairs. (*The hoist moves towards the ledge.*) He's only one weak woodwork teacher – this is – LOOK! – it's fucking eternal hell down there – come unexpected – come early – and coming soon to a place near you – *now get in the fucking hoist!*
(*As the* MAN ON LEDGE *comes blissfully around the corner of the sixth-floor ledge.*)

MAN ON LEDGE: . . . 'The Institute of Social Sciences heard yesterday at its conference in Glasgow that alcoholism is most likely to develop in individuals who have grown up in homes with two lavatories and a budgie . . .'
(*As* SHAUN *arrives on the roof. Approaches the* BRUTES *and the collapsed* MARTIN.)

SHAUN: All right, boys, if you could bring her close personal friend to his feet, if not his senses.

FIRST BRUTE: All right, mate. (*Picks* MARTIN *up with the genuine gentle help of the* SECOND BRUTE.) Nothin' personal, y'know.

SECOND BRUTE: Is right.
(*And the* FIRST BRUTE *realizes that* MARTIN *still has the Tesco bag over his head.*)

MAN ON LEDGE: 'Oxford United have been considering a sponsorship deal with condom firm, Mates, but have pulled out before negotiations reached a climax . . . '

(*The* FIRST BRUTE *tries manfully to tidy* MARTIN's *hair, as* SHAUN *approaches* MARTIN *and takes his wallet out.* MARTIN *flinches.*)

SHAUN: Here y'are. For the discomfort. And a new pair of trousers. (*Thrusts the money at* MARTIN.) Now, off you go, sunbeam.

MARTIN: I'm . . . I'm a . . . I'm a good man.

SHAUN: (*Happily*) Yeah, course y'are, but you see, I'm not.

(MARTIN *stumbles off the roof and down the stairs.* SHAUN *looks out and then down.* MOEY *has got into the hoist. Approaches* MAL *and the* MAN ON LEDGE *as the* MAN ON LEDGE *reaches* MAL. *Looks out at the city. Looks back to* MAL.)

MAN ON LEDGE: Margaret Thatcher, *The Sunday Times* – 'There is no such thing as society' . . . Old Chinese proverb – 'The fish rots from the head down . . . ' *Help. Me.* Help me.

MOEY: I'll help you. I'll find you a toilet. Come on.

MAN ON LEDGE: Will you?

MOEY: Yes.

(MAN ON LEDGE *promptly steps into the hoist.* MOEY *offers his hand to* MAL. *She looks at him. Head bowed, she takes his hand and gets into the hoist.*)

SHAUN: All right, boys, you know what you have to do now.

(*Both* BRUTES *exit.*)

MAN ON LEDGE: (*While attempting to stop himself*) The *Zimbabwe Herald* – 'Mukuviai Wild Life Park – crocodiles are fed every Wednesday afternoon at 4.30. Bring the children.' Oh God, Oh God! What is wrong with me.

(MAL *reaches over to him. Puts her arm around him.*)

MAL: Nothing. Nothing at all. Because you're not wrong.

MOEY: (*To* SHAUN) Eh, I'm going to tell everyone about this.

SHAUN: Yeah, course you are. Now that you think you're nowhere near me.

MOEY: I'll tell them the truth.

(SHAUN *laughs wildly and warmly.*)

SHAUN: *The truth?*

(*While the* MAN ON LEDGE *looks carefully at* MOEY.)

MAN ON LEDGE: Have you ever hit me? At any time?

60

(*The* MAN ON LEDGE *fingers his bandaged head as* SHAUN
begins to speak.)

SHAUN: I know all about the truth, bollocks. Y'can litter the
pavement with the truth – won't work. Not conditioned for
the truth any more. (*Holds the papers aloft for them to see.*) I've
got the truth now – all you're left with is an opinion. And the
world is full of fuckin' opinions!

MAL: Don't – just don't.

MAN ON LEDGE: I think I'm –

MOEY: Fuck it whether it's the truth, opinion or fact. I'm goin'
anyway.

(MOEY *takes hold of the controls. As the proverbial penny drops
for the* MAN ON LEDGE.)

MAN ON LEDGE: I remember now! I remember! I know why I
was up here! (*Turns on* MOEY *in rage.*) And you did hit me,
you fucker!

(*The* MAN ON LEDGE *holds his mouth in shock, but still tries to
get out of the hoist and jump.* MOEY *throws himself on top of
him. They fall to the floor in the hoist, battling.* MOEY *rises from
the floor of the hoist, weary and dishevelled. Looks briefly down.
Aims a kick. Hear a little yelp of pain.* MOEY *takes* MAL'S *hand
off the controls.*)

MOEY: Mal, face facts – he's made a point – people buy the *Sun*
and the *News of the World*. Come on.

(MOEY *moves the hoist away from the building.*)

MAL: No. NO!

(SHAUN *laughs.*)

SHAUN: Goodbye, Mal . . . Mal, I'm free Thursday.

(*The hoist descends.* MAL *raging.*)

MAL: No! No! NO!

(SHAUN *leans over the railings. Relaxes. Lights a cigar. As*
UPSIDE DOWN *and* UPRIGHT *arrive around the corner, as
quickly as they can, holding hands in high anxiety.* UPSIDE
DOWN *and* UPRIGHT *are followed by the* SECOND BRUTE,
closing in with menace. Slowly they reach the FIRST BRUTE *on
the ledge, centre stage. They line up –* FIRST BRUTE, UPSIDE
DOWN, UPRIGHT *and* SECOND BRUTE. *And the* FIRST BRUTE
puts his hand out, palm upwards, to UPSIDE DOWN. *The*

SECOND BRUTE *holds his hand out in the same fashion to*
UPRIGHT. *The* BRUTES *smile and wink.*)

UPRIGHT: (*Bravely, as he looks at the* SECOND BRUTE'*s palm*) I see
a long life, lots of sex and travel, and absolutely no violence
at all.

(*There is a loud explosion from close by. Debris seems to come
scattered from out of the sky around them, as they all, including*
SHAUN, *duck for cover briefly.*)

UPSIDE DOWN: Fuckin' hell, anyone got a hard hat?

(*The* BRUTES *beckon with their hands: 'Hand over the money.'*
UPSIDE DOWN *looks to* UPRIGHT. UPRIGHT *shakes his head
vigorously. The* SECOND BRUTE *takes hold of* UPRIGHT *by the
back of the neck. The* SECOND BRUTE *leans* UPRIGHT *forward
and fast, brings him back.* UPRIGHT *shakes his head even more
vigorously, while the whole of his body shakes as well.*)

SECOND BRUTE: Come 'head, get it over with.

UPRIGHT: I'll get it over with all right – go on, try it – take me –
I've got nothing to lose – take my one chance in life – go on,
try an' take my fuckin' hard-earned money –

FIRST BRUTE: Take the tablets, lad.

SECOND BRUTE: Behave, bollocks – give me the money.

UPRIGHT: Er, no.

BOTH BRUTES: Yes.

UPSIDE DOWN: That feller, he said he didn't want the money.

(*Both* BRUTES *hit the lads in the midriff. Both lads double up.
Both* BRUTES *grab them by the collar.*)

Oh, I see. *You* wanted the money.

UPRIGHT: I've got an ulcer.

(SECOND BRUTE *goes to hit him in the stomach again.*)

But it's in my mouth.

(SECOND BRUTE *raises his hand up.*)

No it isn't –

(UPRIGHT *slumps against the wall, near to tears. The two*
BRUTES *begin to slowly remove the money from the beaten boys'
pockets. A helicopter comes closer. Its searchlight beams on to*
UPRIGHT.)

UPRIGHT: Do y'want to know something? Do y'want to know
something?

FIRST BRUTE: No.

UPRIGHT: . . . I've never wanted a handkerchief so much before in the whole of my fuckin' life . . .

(*The* BRUTES *enjoy counting the money by the side of the boys. Hear a loudspeaker from the helicopter.*)

LOUDSPEAKER: Clear the streets! Clear the streets. Be warned. Go home. Go home!

(SHAUN *laughs. The flames from the city rise higher in the background.*)

SHAUN: . . . Well, I suppose I'll just have to rebuild their hovels for them. At a price. And then the fucking morons can burn them down again.

(*The searchlight swings away from* SHAUN, *the helicopter moves away momentarily.*)

SHAUN: . . . And in the meantime, let them eat stale cakes, give them false dawns and broken dreams, shoddy goods and shitty lives, cheap gin and hard drugs. Let despair and squalor and disease be theirs . . .

(*The helicopter returns. The beam hits* SHAUN. *Closer and closer.* SHAUN *salutes with the Tesco bag.*)

LOUDSPEAKER: Get off the roof! Get off the roof! For your own safety, get off the roof!

(SHAUN *takes his lighter and sets fire to the documents from Tesco bag. He holds it up in the spotlight, much amused. As the flames rise. And his secrets burn as the city burns.*)